G000129982

The Countryman
Book of Humour

The Countryman
Book of Humour

Edited by
MARGARET CAMPBELL

DAVID & CHARLES

NEWTON ABBOT   LONDON
NORTH POMFRET (VT)   VANCOUVER

ISBN 0 7153 7083 9
Library of Congress Catalog Card Number 75-10722

Set in 11 on 13 Photon Plantin
Printed in Great Britain
by Redwood Burn Limited   Trowbridge & Esher
for David & Charles (Holdings) Limited
South Devon House   Newton Abbot   Devon

Published in the United States of America
by David & Charles Inc
North Pomfret   Vermont 05053   USA

Published in Canada
by Douglas David & Charles Limited
132 Philip Avenue   North Vancouver   BC

Contents

Foreword

'It is curious that so few foreigners have noticed that we English are a humorous race,' wrote J. B. Priestley some years ago. It is equally odd that many town dwellers think they possess a superior sense of fun and are entitled to laugh at rather than with their country cousins. Many of the short anecdotes or 'Tail Corn' which have found their way into *The Countyman* since its early days in the 'twenties have depended on this feeling of superiority, making fun of ignorance. I have quoted a few of these in this anthology but more often I have left the last word with the tiller of the soil, like the gardener asked to plant potatoes farther apart: 'Aye, I did that, sir; I planted some in your garden and some in mine.'

Most of the enjoyment in these brief extracts comes from vivid local dialect, like the glen shepherd's description of the new laird: 'Och, he's a wee cratur in a deer-stalker, jist like a moose keekin' oot ablow a bushel.' Or the Berkshire woman, who disturbed some woodlice: 'Oh, I can't abide they chisel-pigs; they makes I criddle all up.'

I have divided the articles and cartoons into the four seasons, though some of the items cover the whole year and much of the 'little measly talk over neighbours' might have been said at any time. Brian Walker's 'Life in a Village' is only marginally autumnal; the British climate being what it is, Hywel's gargoyles in the rain may be relevant in any month. Most of the other cartoons are truly seasonal.

We all, writers included, have our own brand of humour; I have tried to give a varied selection to please the maximum number of readers. Some character studies, for example 'Mothballs', have their share of pathos, which is at the source of much clowning. I only hope that I have interpreted my writers correctly and that they have all meant to be funny. To the best of my knowledge there is, besides Stella Gibbons, only one professional humorist in the collection, H. F. Ellis, who for years enlivened the pages of *Punch*; at least I can be sure of his intentions.

Spring

May day, by Dennis Mallet

These Byways Are Inhabited   by H. F. Ellis

A while ago there was a mild agitation – not the first of its kind – for a national Courtesy Week on the roads. Whether it came to anything, or will have by the time these words are read, I do not at this moment know; nor greatly care. The idea behind such weeks must be that everyone will discover what a nice change it makes and continue in the same for months and years thereafter. What actually happens is that the courteous remain courteous, some few make an ironical parade of the business, taking off their hats and bowing to pedestrians at uncontrolled crossings, and the rest seize such mean advantages as they can and push on. You might as well organise a national No Burglary Week and urge all householders to leave their doors unlocked at night to show confidence and trust.

What did interest me, during the discussions about this Courtesy Week in the newspaper that mooted the plan, was a particularly bland observation (presently to be awarded italics) by one writer on the misbehaviour of local motorists and tractor drivers. He had been quoting some woman correspondent's complaint that men drivers would rarely pull up to let a car out of a side road in the rush hour, and he went on:

> This, I feel, is hardly fair. Most drivers on a major road are prepared to let a car pull out in front of them, if only because one more does not make all that difference. Conversely, one of the worst offenders against good motoring manners on the open road is *the local motorist or tractor driver who pulls out in front of through traffic, and then dawdles along for a hundred yards or so before turning off again.*

Here, unless I gravely misrepresent his attitude, speaks the representative of that great black cloud of motorists who really think that the long-distance driver, *en route* for Rhyl with bucket and spade or Aberystwyth with samples of crockery, has some kind of

superior importance; that through traffic has, or ought to have, the
status of an express train, at whose imperious approach the local
riff-raff should cower in sidings like so many coal trains or cheap
Wednesday excursions. We who live in the country take a different
view. It is true that when we ourselves, once in a while, undertake a
journey of some magnitude, something of the same long-distance
arrogance may come upon us as we sweep into countrysides and
country townships other than our own. It may then seem pretty
intolerable that we, who face the immense task of getting to
Doncaster by nightfall, should be inconvenienced by a man whose
only aim, after pulling out of Willoughby Road, is to turn up
Millstone Lane. But we stop short of aggrandising an irrational
impatience into a divine right.

The plain fact is that the local driver has work to do, or pleasure to
enjoy, not at all less important to him – and perhaps even to the
welfare of the state – than the business or pleasure of the
long-distance motorist. The tractor driver turns into the 'open road'
(whatever that may mean) and off it again, because that is the way
from A to B. He is not to be blamed if the distance is only a hundred
yards; indeed you might have thought the following motorists would
be glad it was no more. And as for 'dawdling along', it ought to be

'Dawdling along'

understood that tractors are not equipped to cruise at sixty m.p.h. Even the best of them cannot accelerate to dizzy speeds and then decelerate again to enter a field within the space of 'a hundred yards or so'. If these simple facts are not clear to motoring correspondents, some of them had better take time off from road-testing Jaguars and try out a Massey Ferguson with a load of mangels in tow.

The point to be remembered, by any long-distance motorists who may be brooding on courtesy as they hew a path through my part of the countryside, is that we who get in their way are at least within our own bailiwick. We live here. The car that turns off so annoyingly down a side road on the right is taking flowers to the church or extra cups to the parish hall. The woman who pulls up at the grocer's does so because she shops there – summer and winter, three hundred days in the year. In our eyes the traffic that streams through *en route* for somewhere else has no superior status whatever. On the contrary: strangers, intruders, second-class citizens, that is what you are. We realise that you have no option, and that you will be as glad as we shall be when the motorway is ready to isolate you in a land where no tractors dawdle and nobody turns left or right from dawn to sunset. But in the meantime kindly remember that you are here on sufferance, and mind your manners.

An American lady who wrote a pleasant book about Oxford some years ago took her title from a remark she overheard in one of the college quadrangles. A small boy, one of a crowd of visitors milling about within the ancient walls, caught sight of a face at some upper window and was startled into speech. 'Dad,' he cried, 'these ruins are inhabited'. Something of the same percipience is required of those who thrust their way along our ancient highways and byways.

There remains to be considered the remarkable statement that 'most motorists on a major road are prepared to let a car pull out in front of them'. Alter 'most' to 'some local' and I might concede a shade of truth to the observation. To get out of the station yard in my country town it is necessary to cross the inward stream of traffic and infiltrate into the outward. At times and seasons when the bulk of the traffic is local, no problem arises. The third or fifth or, on unlucky days, tenth inward driver will flick his lights invitingly, the corresponding outward driver will wave a courteous hand, and there

'Until dizziness and fibrositis supervene'

you are. These drivers, after all, have themselves been penned in the
yard before now and will be again. But when, in whichever direction,
the holidaymakers are pouring through you may turn your head to
right and left, to left and right, until dizziness and fibrositis
supervene, without arousing so much as a flicker of recognition of
your plight. And as for the tractor driver putt-putting at the lane's
end farther out, is there a through motorist in the world who can lay
his hand on the place where his heart should be and declare that he
has ever waved such an obstruction into line ahead? There is not.

It is pleasant to be able to report that the (admittedly local)
courtesy of local motorists proves, on a few weeks' acquaintance, to
be infectious. Moving westwards after many years in London, I was
at first amazed by it ('Can he really mean me to go ahead?') and then
shamed into conformity. I too learned to give way, to flick my
headlights – though not at a car with surfboards on the roof – and to
invite buses to take precedence. One memorable morning, finding the
lane down which I was driving entirely blocked by a great throng of
people on foot and a-horse, leaning on bicycles or sitting on
Land-Rovers, I neither blew my horn nor made any kind of protest. I
merely got out and lit my pipe and went and rested my elbows on a
gate to see what the harriers were up to. I was a countryman now,
with country manners, experiencing the warm glow that comes with

'You're blocking the road'

a consciousness of civilised behaviour, patience and courteous consideration for others. Through motorists would be astonished to find how agreeable the sensation is.

The outcome of this small incident was not altogether satisfactory. A huntsman, perhaps even the master, rode up after a while and said, from his considerable eminence: 'Is that thing yours? Get it out of the way, will you? You're blocking the road'. I had much to say to this man in reply. I had to tell him that, far from blocking the road, I was myself being blocked; that by waiting patiently and without rancour until his infernal hounds moved on I was exhibiting a typical country courtesy that called for thanks, not a reprimand. But these things went unsaid for, like all mounted men, he did not stay for an answer. He simply issued his commands and clattered imperiously away.

The arrogance of local horsemen is, however, too extensive a subject to be dealt with here.

Drawings by A. S. Graham

The Season of the Year   by Arnold Wiles

'See what I mean? It's no use writing to Martha for a couple of weeks yet'

'It's getting too much iron'

'You might like to mend this hammock while you're patching my gardening trousers'

You Can't Miss It   by Peter Fisher

'No,' said the woman with the pram, 'there ain't no farmer o' that name round these parts. Tell you what though; there's a farm down this road an' someone there might know.' I was looking for Joe Brown of Yew Tree Farm and, knowing that it must be close by, I drove into the first farmyard. There I met Joe himself. 'Knew you'd find it all right', he said; 'everybody for miles knows me.' There was no name on the gate, and I forbore to mention that the three people I had asked along the way all professed never to have heard of him. There was no yew tree to be seen either; that had been cut down the day after his father lost six heifers with yew poisoning.

Joe Brown is right, of course; all his friends know where he lives, and others soon learn. If he were to put the name of the farm on the gate it would only encourage oil-and-cattle-cake travellers, not to mention the animal-medicine men. Most of his neighbours' farms remain equally anonymous, except for that of the odd man who advertises eggs, bed-and-breakfast or chickens, and of the pedigree breeder who proclaims the home of a prize-winning herd.

For the man who has to seek these places by day or night, this fine sturdy indifference is difficult to deal with at first. He tends to allow too little time between calls and is forever apologising for late arrival. Failure to find his destination when all his guides have assured him, 'You can't miss it', gives him a sense of inferiority. Perhaps, after a quarter of a century spent in searching for men or places that seem never to have existed, I can pass on a few of the lessons I have learnt.

My opening paragraph shows that I sometimes break my own rules, the first of which is: 'Never ask a woman with a pram'. In the first place she doesn't know, and in the second she is afraid you will wake the baby, so she will say anything to get rid of you. In general the only people worth asking for directions are roadmen and postmen. Policemen tend to be new to the district, old men are often stone deaf, and the smartly dressed man is 'only down for the day at my daughter's place'. In summer, of course, the hazards multiply, and the knowledgeable native is harder to trace. Perhaps it is better then to make for the post office, where directions – and potted biographies – are available when trade is dull.

'Perhaps it is better then to make for the post office'

Another rule is that any resemblance between the name of the farm and its external appearance is at best coincidental. The oldest inhabitant will tell you that he does not remember even a tree at Cherry Orchard Farm, and they have cut down the elms at Elm Tree Farm and flogged them in the town at £4 10s the ton while they were green. The New Inn lost its licence twenty years ago, but the house still bears that name. When townees buy a house in the country they often change the name to something like Shangri-la or Clovelly without telling the locals, so that at weekends droves of their friends scour the district, vainly searching for their rural retreat. The natives cannot help much, as they still call the place Starvelark Cottage and will continue to do so, even when a succession of owners have changed the name to Hillview, Honeysuckle Villa and Pevensey.

A good rule is to obtain a one-inch-to-the-mile Ordnance Survey map of the area you intend to travel. If you are fortunate enough to have a companion who can read a map, so much the better; if not, you should pause now and again at a cross-roads or other landmark and check your bearings. Don't be like the army officer who stopped a policeman of my acquaintance in mid Wales during the war, when

'Pause now and again'

the signposts had been taken down, and asked him to point out their
whereabouts on his map. The policeman looked at it and said
gravely, 'Can't be done, sir'. Taken aback, the officer demanded
sharply, 'Why not?' 'You are not on that map, sir', was the reply. The
officer had piloted his chauffeur for fifty miles in the wrong direction
before asking his way.

There may be some psychological explanation for the curious
tendency, even among apparently normal passers-by, to deny all
knowledge of the place you are seeking. 'Never heard of it' is the
abrupt answer, though further questioning sometimes elicits a
grudging admission that the place does exist; and when you arrive at
your destination you are told that the reluctant informant is an old
acquaintance who passes the house daily. Another peculiarity, about
which all regular travellers are in agreement, is that inner urge
which compels them to stop and speak to any pedestrian afflicted in
some way not at first apparent; he may have a vocal impediment, be
stone deaf or mentally unsound. Amid much embarrassment the
red-faced motorist is then glad to escape in any direction.

In different parts of the country different conventions apply, and
none more so than in Wales. If your Welsh pronunciation is weak,

write the name of the farm on a piece of paper and ask any passer-by. 'Trefach,' he reads, 'is it Trefach Uchaf, Trefach Isaf, or Trefach Ganol?' James, you remark hopefully, is the farmer's name. 'Two of them are James', he replies; 'they are some relation of yours perhaps, and have you come far?' When he has extracted your history and your business, he will direct you most exactly with wide sweeps of his arms: 'Go past Caersalem, turn left on a square by Bethesda, and the road is a small bit past Gerizim'. The 'square', by the way, means a cross-roads. But take note of his hands, and if he tells you to turn right while his left hand is executing a circling motion, follow the hand, for that is always correct. His opposite number in England will direct you by pub names, but the ubiquitous chapels are more convenient in Wales, situated as they so often are at cross-roads.

One Welsh complication is that your man may not be known by his proper name – David Davies perhaps – but as Dai Penwennol, to distinguish him from Dai Shop-isaf and Dai Come-again. Sometimes the nickname is so deeply engraved in local custom that acquaintances express surprise when they hear the real name,

'No matter how heavily the rain is falling'

perhaps for the first time in years. One endearing characteristic of
the Welsh is that no matter how heavily the rain is falling, they will
stand and explain your route at great length. This is rather typical of
hill-men everywhere.

In Scotland you may be given casual directions to a spot thirty
miles distant as if it were a mile or two down the glen. In the
north-east, however, they have a charming habit of putting up a sign
at the farm entrance, bearing the name, with carvings of the
livestock kept there. Thus the sign may read 'Howe of Garten' with
carvings of Aberdeen-Angus cattle, Rhode Island Red hens and
Cheviot sheep above. You are tempted to go down the lane, though
you have no business there, and shake the farmer's hand for his
thoughtfulness and artistry.

In parts of Ireland, too, one can enjoy being directed, knowing full
well that one will probably lose the point of the conversation while
trying to commit to memory some of the verbal felicities in which it
abounds. My favourite recollection is of the old man who was telling
me how to find a farm at Ballynahinch, nearly thirty miles away:
'You know where the old toll gates used to be? No? Well, it's half a

On the way to Ballynahinch

mile this side of that, near five road-ends, down an old loaning'. Road-ends are cross-roads in Ulster, and a loaning is a lane.

Stevenson, who was well acquainted with the subject, once remarked that it was better to travel hopefully than to arrive, and on another occasion that he travelled for travel's sake. There is much to be said for this attitude, but one must put forward a case for a definite objective; otherwise there would be little excuse for stopping the roadman or postman with a request for directions. They, on the other hand, would not be able to demonstrate their peculiar and extensive knowledge of the topography of the next parish but two. And what can contribute more to an inner glow of satisfaction than to direct a stranger through a maze of by-roads and hamlets to a particularly well concealed little cottage, and to see him on his way with a final, 'You can't miss it'?

Drawings by Sheila Walker

Portrait of a House   by Jane Connard

Over my mantelpiece hangs the portrait of a house. A steep-roofed, rambling building, it stands back behind a group of beech trees that go right up out of the picture. Behind the trees is a typical East Anglian sky; a bright blue that is quickly being obliterated by stormy clouds. A strong wind shakes the cherry blossom in the foreground. Little Sutton House, caught in sunlight on a blustery, late spring day. My father's hands must have got very cold while he recorded it all so lovingly, seated on a camp stool among the cabbages!

As I look at the picture, tiny incidents pop up in my memory. Father: gallantly setting off down the lane on his bicycle; folding easel, paint box and camp stool strapped on the carrier, and a fair-sized canvas tied on his back; the struggle to mount – then triumph as he whizzed along, the brisk wind behind him converting the canvas into a sail; then the inevitable, sudden collapse when he tried to steer the bicycle round a sharp bend in the lane against the wind. Father: enraged by some trivial incident on a dull wet day that kept him indoors, attacking an ornate mahogany sideboard with a

Little Sutton House by Philip Connard R.A., the painting which inspired
this article

saw and cutting off an ear-shaped ivy leaf that he disapproved of; but
the wood proving very tough and his rage having abated, he could
not be bothered to saw off its pair. Father and Mother helping us to
carry camp beds and bedding out under the beech trees on a hot May
night, so that we could lie in bed and look up at the silky, translucent
leaves, and listen to the nightingales singing in the hazel bushes after
dark.

The house faces south-west. Standing at the window one can see
heathland, sloping meadows, larch plantations, true woodland and a
tidal river, all in one turn of the head. And then, beyond the river
rises the town of Woodbridge, with the flint church tower at the
summit. How my parents came to hear that this house was standing
empty I do not know. My sister and I had hardly heard it mentioned
before we found ourselves transplanted there, with wild enthusiasm
and inadequate furniture. Had my mother controlled her impatience

and waited for a surveyor's report before moving us, had she even read the agreement, she might have drawn back. Thank goodness she did not.

Huge beech trees beside the gate, a shrubbery of lilac and syringa, arches of old-fashioned cluster roses, a wide lawn ending in a row of great walnut trees, an orchard with a carpet of snowdrops to relieve the misery of early spring, a splendid asparagus bed, a hazel copse where the nightingales nested every summer – the list of delights was inexhaustible.

But some of the floors were collapsing with dry rot, and the drains were in such a lethal state that we children were immediately sent away to friends while they were being re-laid. The electric lighting plant and the central heating mentioned by the agent did not work, the lawn was a huge swamp and the walnut trees were dying. Too late my parents found they were responsible for all repairs. But Father had only just recovered from shell-shock, and this move had been planned to help him regain his composure and peace of mind!

Because she had been so imprudent, Mother defended herself by building up a picture of the unscrupulous landlady who had lured us on into a fool's paradise. On the contrary, the woman could not keep us out! But after the trauma of the first few weeks, Mother's choice was vindicated; Little Sutton was the most lyrically delightful place I have ever lived in.

My mother's sister came to join us, and filled the handsome stables with a herd of goats. These were a constant source of irritation to Father, who objected to the frequent escapes that took place, and to the smell of goat muck on my aunt's clogs. She was absent-minded, and sometimes forgot to take them off before coming in to breakfast.

We seemed to live in a constant state of excitement provided by the goats and their escapades, the doves we kept in a chicken house, the farmyard and its smelly cage of undulating ferrets. Even shopping expeditions were an adventure, as we had to cross the river by ferry-boat to avoid a cycle ride of many miles. The walk to the ferry may have taken only about twenty minutes but to children it seemed longer. The footpath was only kept trodden by ourselves, and in the winter the stickiness of the soil, in summer the lack of shade and the high stinging nettles, made this an exhausting walk. There was a feeling of relief when we reached the woodland where there was shelter from the wind, and velvety moss on which we loved to run in and out of the trees. Then the path sloped steeply downhill to a little hard, where we waited for the ferryman from the Woodbridge shore.

Behind the house ran a lane, quite a narrow track with rank-smelling elder trees forming a tunnel. As the track ascended the hill these bushes gave way to gorse and the track itself became completely sandy, the banks on each side covered with soft turf dotted with rabbit droppings. At the top of the rise one was on a wide heath, flat except for some large, smooth mounds. We enjoyed exercising the more docile of the goats on these mounds. We would tear up to the top, hauling the goats after us, and then run down the other side as fast as possible. The goats enjoyed it too, prancing with their elegant legs over the then undreamed of wealth of the Sutton Hoo burial ship. We were so near it; we even played and jumped on it, not knowing what lay beneath our feet.

This was the only time in my childhood when my parents had a fairly stable domestic staff. We had a gardener, young and rather handsome, a cook, and a land girl to help look after the goats. Mother hated running a house, and she loved singing, dancing, and acting. She soon discovered that our pretty, demure cook, Daisy, had a remarkably sweet singing voice, and that her young man who lived nearby played the accordion. The gardener's mother knew a lot of Suffolk folk songs, and the land girl also liked singing. In this remote house, long before the days of radio, television and easy transport, there was a need for home-made amusement, and Mother's enthusiasm soon established a custom of 'Wednesday Evenings'. Our staff, and their friends and relations, would come to the house, assemble in the largest room – which happened to be a very large, brick-floored back kitchen – and spend the evening dancing to the music of Reggie's accordion, learning country dances and singing any songs they knew. Mrs Lennard's folk songs were extremely bawdy, but to this Mother made no objection. The audacity with which she swept them into sharing her amusements seems almost incredible. I think she succeeded because she so needed them in order to enjoy these pursuits herself. Had people of her own class lived near at hand, they would have been swept in as well.

My sister Helen and I loved the Wednesdays; we were very unsophisticated, and were not afraid that Mother was being 'peculiar'. A year or two later when we had been to boarding school and had met other children, we would have recoiled. But at this time we loved the dancing, the accordion, and handing round iced buns with the tea at nine o'clock. Father frowned upon these proceedings. It annoyed him intensely to hear Mother accompanying Daisy in 'Songs of Araby' when Daisy should have been cooking the lunch. But he had to agree that she sang delightfully. He was furious, and the house rocked with his rage, when Mother let herself in for producing *A Midsummer Night's Dream,* with the inevitable dislocation of domestic routine. But at the last minute he came forward to help, and arranged a set and lighting that raised the production into something quite unexpected and remarkable in the way of amateur theatricals.

As well as having a lovely voice, Daisy was a good cook, and it was a hard blow when eventually she left. Good cooks were hard to find, and harder still to keep in a house a mile from the road. Christmas was approaching, and my grandfather was coming to spend it with us. He was a melancholy clergyman who had retired because of failing health and eyesight, who felt the cold badly and had a delicate digestion. Mother dreaded the visit. Then, just before he was due to arrive, she heard of a Mrs Cooper. Through what channel this paragon was washed up on our shore I cannot remember; I only remember that she gave us the Christmas of our lives.

She arrived very quickly after hearing of the situation. No sooner had Mother mentioned that she might be coming than she was on the doorstep with her luggage. We welcomed her as though she were the Herald Angel himself. She was forty-ish, good-looking and extremely cheerful. She had the natural sociability of the born hotel manageress. She also had great tact, never letting her jollity pass beyond the bounds of the appropriate, but cheering even Grandpa with her briskness, her gaiety and her magnificent cooking. She was determined that Mother should have a good time, and took her up cups of tea in bed. Nothing was too much trouble.

We adored her. The whole household, including Father, went about in a state of euphoria. I think that at no time in my mother's married life was she so unharassed, or Father so good-tempered, as during the reign of Mrs Cooper. Christmas Day and the Christmas dinner was a triumph. Mrs Cooper carried in the feast with an air, wearing a sprig of mistletoe, and had she offered to embrace my grandfather I think he might have been well pleased! Shortly after his departure we all went up to London for a spree. On our return the following day we were dismayed to find no Mrs Cooper. She had completely vanished. Almost immediately we were visited by the police. We were surprised to hear that she was not really Mrs Cooper – she was a Mrs Ward, wanted for running a brothel in Woodbridge and receiving stolen goods. Because she so genuinely liked Mrs Cooper, Mother was grieved to find that her only valuable rings were missing. But she was not angry or outraged: she felt that Mrs Cooper had pretty well earned them by making us all so happy and good-tempered, if even for so short a time.

By degrees the house deteriorated beyond the point where it was habitable. Dry rot was corrupting the house room by room, and when the gap in the stairs became so wide that even my agile and spirited mother could no longer leap across it, the time had come to leave. My sister and I wept passionate tears. We lay in bed plotting and weeping. We would grow up and earn enough money to buy the house from the rotten landlady – we would never, never be reconciled to living anywhere else.

Of course we were. But we never forgot; and I think that all my life, in choosing each house that I have lived in, I have been trying to reassemble the golden ingredients of those few years.

'After all, if you have a pet, you might as well enjoy its company'

Restrictive practice

by Siggs

Shooting a Line   by Frederick Street

With a cable across one field and a transformer in another, I was not feeling exactly co-operative when the Electricity Board asked if they could run a line across a third; and when I discovered they wanted to put four poles in less than four acres I stuck my toes in. There was rebellion in the air, for it was not long since a local farmer had threatened to dismantle a pylon with his own personal spanner if it were erected on his land. Also the Board had not taken the trouble to draw a new map to send me, so I could see they had originally intended to run the line across a neighbour's field; he had obviously said 'No' and meant it. Not long before, I had won a minor victory by forcing them to follow the line of a hedge instead of cluttering up the field and landscape; so I was spoiling for a fight.

I began by sparring in civil service style, playing for time; 'Dear Sir — Kindly note that your map is out of date. The course of the stream was altered in 1944 and is now approximately as shown on the plan in pencil. Will you please replot this in order that the whole effect of the new line may be considered?' Not that it mattered where the stream was; but it left me with the advantage. I followed with a request that the positions of any poles be marked on the plan. This could have been included in the first letter, of course, but the full effect would have been lost.

When the plan came back a second time with the positions of the poles and the line marked on it, I made a tactical error: I tried the same trick twice, suggesting that the line should be rerouted along a footpath. I thought I could quote the precedent of the last line of their least resistance, not knowing that it would involve a right-angled turn where the lane reached my southern boundary. The possible expense brought a personal visit from an official — something I had wanted to avoid.

I do not know whether you have ever had a visit from a wayleave officer — the Electricity Board's name, I believe, for their professional charmers. I lost out at once on the plan to follow the lane. When the extra cost was explained to me I felt little better than a smart financier doing a sharp deal that would seriously threaten the pound; but I was not quite finished. There were still the sordid financial details. The statutory rate for a single pole on arable land is five shillings a year, which is paid after income tax has been deducted at the full rate, bringing it down to about three shillings. What, I asked, was I expected to do with the twelve bob I received as rent for the four poles? Was I to give it to the tractor-driver to compensate him for the trouble it would cause him? And did the Board know that a single obstruction in a field could cause hours of extra work and produce a torrent of strong Anglo-Saxon words? The field was often planted with potatoes, and I described all the work that would be involved in planting and digging by hand. The area round each pole would also become a breeding ground for couch-grass. All this, I submitted, was worth not less than £25 a year.

Regretfully my visitor agreed with me: he sympathised, tut-tutted about the tractor-driver, and pursed his lips in an expression of combined horror and understanding when I mentioned the couch-grass. Quietly and persistently he explained . . . there was an Act of Parliament . . . assessed by the district valuer . . . would need another Act to change the rate.

Then I made my last desperate move. 'All right,' I said, 'I don't seem to stand a chance; but just tell me why a new line is needed.'

'It is entirely for the benefit of local people', I was assured. 'We have had so many complaints about the poor supply that we must do something.'

I signed quickly, thanked him for his trouble, apologised for making difficulties, hoped he understood and was sure he was busy, but to let me know if the men wanted any help when they came to do the work. A little non-plussed by my change of attitude, he walked away with the slightly dazed air of a man who has just got out of a cold bath.

Everyone had been having trouble. My electric pump worked fast enough to provide only a trickle; people who cooked by electricity had had to wait until three o'clock for their Sunday dinner, and our television screens were superimposed with a series of white graphs on grey backgrounds. And I was the organiser of the round robin which had now come home to roost on the wires to be provided.

Bluebell Time

by Arnold Wiles

'That's good bluebells you've ruined!'

'Forgot to shut the gate'

'So glad you like my bluebells. I'm partial to tulips myself'

Wayleaves   **by Stanley G. Bennett**

For more than forty years, as a wayleave officer, I had to interview owners and tenants of property for permission to erect telegraph poles. Much of my work was in Cotswold villages, and I had great sympathy for the people who lived there and did not wish to see poles in the main thoroughfares. Even though consent had been given by the highway authority it was often possible, when an objection was made, to arrange with local owners to site the fixtures out of view in back lanes and similar places.

Most people were accommodating, but I met with some strange objections. A geologist refused to have three poles in his hedgebank 'because they would be on a ridge of oolitic conglomerate'. An elderly lady would not accept a wire stay in her garden because she was certain lightning would strike it and destroy her thatched cottage. A doctor, when signing an agreement for a small cable to be placed on his house, added the words, 'providing that it does not interfere with any of the five senses'. Once I was sent to a Cotswold cottage to interview a London woman who had written to the Postmaster General objecting to wires crossing her garden. When I introduced myself she said, 'I expected the Postmaster General to call', and slammed the door in my face.

Not all wayleaves were obtained by gift of speech; sometimes I had to work for them. One farmer said, 'Just turn the handle of the grindstone while I sharpen this hedging hook'. Another, fearing that his end was near, was anxious to make a will; and as I had spent some years in a lawyer's office, I was able to help him. My reward was his consent to place fourteen wire stays in fields planted with wheat and almost ready for cutting.

I had sometimes to obtain permission to cut trees, and in this I encountered a few obstacles. The value placed on them varied considerably. One owner of a crab-apple in a hedge readily agreed that 'the damned thing' should be not only trimmed but cut right down; but his neighbour would not allow a crab to be touched, because he could sell the fruit at £2 a pot for jelly. Three elderly maiden sisters objected to the trimming of an old horse-chestnut that was interfering with wires, and the route had to be diverted.

Shouting into an ancient ear-trumpet to a trio of women who were both adamant and stone-deaf defeated me.

An irate landowner who did not receive his wayleave payment on the day it was due instructed his men to cut down four spans of wire; these he sent with his compliments to the office of the engineers. Another owner, who was refused wayleave payment for poles which carried his own circuit, threatened to cut down a whole line on his land. When he arrived on the site with handsaw and axe he discovered that the poles were not the usual wooden ones, but steel joists erected during the war-time timber shortage.

What's for a Penny? by Kathleen Gooding

Our store stands high in the Wye Valley, with panoramic views and a rose-garden in front. Offa's Dyke crosses just below. Every morning between a quarter past eight and nine o'clock the children arrive by three converging roads, to buy sweets on their way to school. We try to keep up with the times. We have frozen foods and a refrigerator and, being a country store, nearly everything else, including hardware, boots, weekly papers, medicines, fruits and groceries. None of this matters to our young shoppers. They gravitate to the sweet counter with the unanimity of driver ants.

'What have you got that's new?' is the sixty-four-dollar question. I work hard to answer it, seeking new confectionery delights; but experience has taught me that some sweets live for ever, others but a day. I court bankruptcy if I deal too heavily in popcorn, for instance. Like marbles and whip-and-top, it has its season and thereafter is deader than last year's Christmas card.

'What have you got for a penny?' is another challenge. There is no inflation in the child world; a penny is still an important and respectable coin of the realm. I have black jacks at four a penny, fruit salads, gobstoppers, refreshers (orange, lemon, banana and strawberry flavours), aniseed balls, comfits and sherbet swags. A fine old sweet that children of all ages love with grandmother is the peppermint, black or brown, clear or opaque. For boys, particularly, there is chewing-gum. They are noisy, well informed and addicted.

'Good for your teeth. A dentist said it in the paper. I read it.' There are also high-quality penny bars of milk chocolate, which good mothers buy; no child ever buys one for himself.

'Would you like a little piece of good butterscotch?' I inquire occasionally, to do my mite towards their training. 'No thanks. It makes my teeth ache. Haven't you got a twopenny slab of treacle toffee?' Of course, toffee never makes the teeth ache.

With twopence new horizons are opened. There are love hearts (six colours), pink nougat, sweet cigarettes, jelly babies, bootlaces, chews, everlasting strips, Tom Thumb mixtures, dolly mixtures, roast ducks with new potatoes and green peas, wine gums (port, burgundy and claret) and many others. For threepence the variety is endless; it would, if they wished, buy good fruit drops or barley sugar. But even at sixpence most children prefer the romantic coloured sweet to the quality one. 'Fudge? No thank you. Mum buys that. I'll have a quarter of rainbow sherbet and a sucker, please.'

The jolliest thing is the 'lucky bag' filled with sweets and a toy. It may be a traffic signal with a tiny switch to bring red, green and amber disks into view, or a plastic pool of coloured fish, or one of a hundred more. You pays your threepence and you takes your choice of a yellow or magenta bag. When fingers are too weak with excitement, teeth will rip it open. The bags are firm favourites with small Johnny; but selling him sweets is an occupational hazard.

'I can't find my money.' Together we shake, bang, slap and feel in pockets. 'It must have slipped into the lining.' He starts to undress, then remembers; 'I stuffed it into the peak of my cap.' Now we can get down to business.

'Got anything really nice this morning? It's Thursday.'

'What's wrong with Thursday?'

'It's Nature day. I don't like Nature. We're having stamens and pollen till playtime.' He is gloomy. 'I think I'd better have a lucky bag for before and some raspberry sherbet to turn my milk pink for after.' And off he goes to drown his sorrows in pink milk.

Children are good shoppers; they like to take their time and obtain value. Generally, for their sakes and mine, I keep my watch a shade fast and refer to it occasionally while they dither and haver over the last halfpenny. 'They'll be singing the first hymn,' I say to them.

'Will you have some sweet tobacco or a jelly strip?'

'What did you have Mary?' says the undecided one to her chum waiting by the door.

'I had whoppas. But they're twopence and you've only got a penny,' says Mary, and we are back where we started. I know how politicians feel at disarmament conferences. Then suddenly she settles for the jelly strip and goes off, swopping half of it with Mary for half of the whoppa and getting the best of both worlds.

Fashions count in sweets. One day last year we had a new line: an 'outer' with sweets of many hues and a plastic bucket for measuring them. For a penny we filled the bucket to the brim and emptied the contents into a brightly coloured bag. The cry went abroad, 'A bucket of sweets for a penny at the shop.' It was fifteen minutes to nine. I looked through the window. The whole school seemed to be pouring down the road. Highly alarmed I whipped behind my counter, got ready my measuring bucket and lived through the fastest-moving quarter of an hour of my life. But I have not repeated the line: it was altogether too exciting, and perhaps next time, like the popcorn, it would be an anticlimax.

Coming to Terms with The Environment   by H. F. Ellis

Years ago, when my own environment was a play-pen, or its Edwardian equivalent, with a couple of small flannel waistcoats airing on one side of it, there was a general belief that every organism had its environment and was affected by it. Moths had one, and became noticeably melanistic if there was a lot of soot about. At this time, too, heredity was a word much bandied about outside the confines of my nursery. Some said that inherited characteristics were more influential and enduring than those developed in and by an individual's surroundings; others said not.

Just when the environment got its definite article I am unable to say. It must have been round about the time that facilities and amenities began to spring up and proliferate in this already overcrowded island. Facilities for recreation, reading, worship, washing and so on took the place of old-fashioned football grounds, libraries, churches etc., and very soon began to group themselves into

Amenities by a process akin, it may be, to osmosis. For a man already far gone in middle age it was not easy to adjust to these ameliorations. The concept of adjustment itself was hardly more than embryonic in my formative years. My old nurse, for instance, when she made some irksome change in my environment (a sailor suit, perhaps), never included 'You must learn to adjust to new pressures, Master H.' among her innumerable wise saws and encouraging maxims. Still, I made some attempt as time went by to bring order and method, at least in my own mind, into a situation of increasing complexity and actually got to work on the construction of a kind of statistical table, viz.:

> Six facilities equal one amenity;
> Twelve amenities constitute one planned environment;
> Twenty-four planned environments bid fair to attain conurbation status.

If this scheme had gained general acceptance it might have done something to keep the growth of the Environment within bounds. But the idea came too late. In a go-ahead country like ours, where the shilling is dead and the spectre of metrication looms well above the offing, my table had altogether too duodecimal a ring. There was also an infestation at about this time of Neighbourhoods, Precincts (hitherto only encountered in stories about New York cops) and Vertically Integrated Concepts, which were difficult to fit into any comprehensive numerical scheme. Heredity remained reasonably constant, but with the Environment it was becoming daily more arduous to keep in touch. Offshore rigs, to my astonishment, were sunk in it; and to evaluate the influence of these tripods on my characteristics, as compared with my father's genes, was entirely beyond my compass. In my bewilderment I took refuge, I am ashamed to say, in a return to childhood and began to scribble nursery rhymes all over my writing amenities, e.g.

> How many metres to Babylon?
> Five thousand six hundred and thirty-one score and ten.
> Can I get there by North Sea Gas?
> Yes. Facilities for conversion from candlelight are obtainable
> on application in BLOCK CAPITALS to the
> Amenity Controller and his charismatic men.

Meanwhile the Environment was growing apace. By 1969 it had utterly abandoned its old role of blackening the wings of moths and was not conterminous with the British Isles and their surrounding seas. By 1970 it was lapping the shores of the United States. Inevitably, instead of influencing others it became itself subject to almost intolerable pressures. Things were thrown into it. 'An estimated 160 million pounds of mercury', declared *The Times* in a Christmas message about poisoned fish, 'has been dumped in the environment this century.' The boot was now on the other leg with a vengeance. With its mastery over human and animal life almost entirely gone, the Environment had become something to be saved, and the British Government, in what looked like a last desperate throw, appointed a Secretary of State for it.

This was a far cry from flannel waistcoats and the old snug personal cocoon to which everyone, moth or man, used to have a right. Nothing seemed to be left to blame for one's own individual failures or successes, happiness or misery, but poor old neglected heredity – for which at the moment of writing not even a Royal Commission has been appointed.

The hideous thing, one of the hideous things, about this new Environment is that it is so convenient. Indeed, it may have been touch and go whether we had a Minister for the Convenience. 'The Environment' is all-embracing – except that it has no people in it. There is no need to define what you are talking about. There is the word, a nice, solid, official-sounding sort of word, and something must obviously correspond with it. It is the kind of word that goes well with cost-benefit analyses. It saves the endless fatigue of acquainting yourself with all the minutiae that make up the countryside, all the real personal environments that constitute the stuff of life. It is as handily soulless as, for instance, that Area 26 into which a part of my own county is to be gloriously translated ('Come on, Area 26', I hear myself shouting at some inter-environmental Rugby football match of the future. 'Shove this damned Conurbation off it!'). It is too grandiose a conception, stuffed as it is with mercury and oil-rigs, to concern itself with what matters to us, here in a small village that does not even boast an Environment Officer.

What does matter, environmentally, to the individual? There

The Rising Sap   **Arnold Wiles in garden shops**

'Do you realise that we've spent £1.15 on plants and seeds, and £4.55 on fertiliser and pesticides?'

'I'm looking for something quick-growing that will smother an acre of ground overnight'

'. . . halfway up the garden path – covered with roses . . .'

'It certainly sounds impressive, but it looks pretty insignificant to me for 75 pence'

reached me, rather surprisingly, some months ago a letter from
Lincoln First Banks, Inc., of Rochester, N.Y. (addressed to me as 'a
member of the communications industry' – which is no bad thing to
be; old members, Shakespeare and Tolstoi, to name but two).
'Lincoln First Banks', they singularly wrote, 'is very much concerned
about tomorrow and has undertaken a serious study into the
American life styles which might be anticipated in the 1980s. The
objective of the research has been to look at *the individual* 10 years
from now *and all of the forces affecting him to make up his total
environment.*'

This was cheering. Here was an organisation prepared, as is clear
from the words I have taken the liberty of italicising, to recognise the
existence of individuals, each with his own environment, and to show
confidence, what is more, that the same state of affairs would last for
at least another decade. And how did Lincoln First Banks define or
classify the 'forces affecting'?

'The study profile', they wrote, 'was divided into 12 sub-topics –
The Qualitative Life Style; Population; Employment; Sustenance;
Housing and Construction; Transportation and Communication;
Health; Education; Social Structures; Ecology; Government;
Culture/Recreation/Entertainment.'

Well, that adds up to quite an environment. Obviously very
different from that formless expanding affair with the definite
article, to which I take such grave exception. Even so it does not
sound quite the personal environment I hanker after. It is not cosy
enough. It lacks warmth. I have difficulty in squeezing into any of
the twelve categories some of the forces that particularly affect me
here. We have Transportation in the village, and Government
naturally, and Social Structures, if that is what the Parish Hall is;
but it is none of these that has incised the calipers so deeply from my
nose to my chin. It is old Mrs Barstow and her dogs. Nor can my
characteristic (certainly not inherited) of darting down side roads
whenever Colonel Curtis comes along be properly entered under
Recreation.

What I am trying to say is that, if Lincoln First Banks were to
extend their survey across the Atlantic and happened to call at my
house for information, the details of my environment that I should
wish to stress, the forces that really affect me for good or ill, would

not fit very readily into their Study Profile – or that of any other praiseworthy sociologist. Ground elder could, I suppose, come at a pinch under Ecology, but to attempt to subsume the milkman's gay errors under Sustenance or Mrs Barstow under Culture or Entertainment, either now or in ten years' time, would be to make a mockery of serious research. Or is it possible that both these dear people, and the rats in the outhouse, and the view from my bedroom window, and the gurglings made by our vertically disintegrated central-heating system, and Matins, and Colonel Curtis, and the delicious row in the Debating Society, and a hundred other vital ingredients in the environment of myself and my neighbours all make up our Qualitative Life Style?

I cannot say; as yet, for all our amenities, we have no such thing in the village. What I can say is that this sort of personal and priceless environment is not going to be saved, or even comprehended, by any Secretary of State, born or unborn. We have to do that ourselves.

Settin' This Un Out   **by John Miller**

I'll set along o' you gel, if you don't mind me by.
Now there en't no call to move gel, there's a mort o' room for I.
I en't much of a goo at talkin', but I reckon I'll 'ave a try
For there's summat I got to say to you now; an' I'll tell 'ee for why.

If I 'ad as many shillin's as the times I've seen you round,
I'll lay that'd pay for a farm'ouse an' a tidy owd bit o' ground.
For I were born 'ere; an' you come arter not two year I'll be bound,
So that make nigh on eighteen year you bin in sight an' sound.

That's a queer owd do but me an' you we en't 'ad a word to share
Since we come outer school an' I played the fool an' cow-de-dunged
    your hair.
An' my owd mum she tanned my bum as 'ard as she bloomin' well
    dare;
An' you 'ad to set bi yourself for a bit, but I couldn't set me nowhere.

That smell nice now though, soft an' all; so p'r'aps that done un
   good.
As I were a-sayin', that's curious like as me an' you's a-stood
Come winter an' summer for all they years like a couple o' trees in a
   wood;
One givin' no more'n a nod to the t'other. I don't reckon that's good.

Now I en't a-speakin' for you gel, 'cus you might not be of a mind,
But that come to me jest lately-like as how I bin a bit blind,
An 'ull very like miss me bacon for chewin' too long at the rind.
An' that's as true as I sit, what you don't git cut you wun't git to
   grind.

Now if you don't feel as you'd like to, that's up to you to say,
But I wouldn't be off to be seen about wi' the likes o' you one day.
So if you'd like to give it a try mate you wun't goo far astray;
An' if that don't come right − why, you'll find plenty more sticks in
   the hedge, I'll lay.

Spring Tail Corn

CHESHIRE woman, showing her garden: 'I've lived wi' flowers all
me life, but I dunna want 'em on me when I'm gone. I should kick
'em off. I want to be cremated, but our Alf 'angs fire'.

NORTH COUNTRY man's greeting: 'Well, Bill, oo' today, are ta
feeling gay well o' oor alike?'

BERKSHIRE description of a tight-fisted couple: 'There they sits,
one one side of the fire and one t'other, holding on to two sides of a
sixpence and stretching on 'im to make 'n go as fur as a shilling.'

DENTIST to old farmer patient: 'I didn't know your daughter was
married'. 'Her inna.' 'Well, whose baby is she minding over the road
there?' 'Mine.' 'You're not serious?' 'Oh ah. The owd 'ooman sparked
up agen.'

OLD FARMER, discussing bad winters of the past in the pub, 'Ah, six wi'ks of frost and snow we 'ad – and all in March.'

ODD-JOB man in Dorset, recounting tale of hen that had killed her chicks: 'Aah, she were a vierce, viery vowl, she were'.

HAMPSHIRE village gossip: 'She buzzes round the village like a dumble dore in a poppy head.' (A dumble dore is a bumble bee.)

FARMER, a school manager, after inspecting a very rural infant's school, 'They were sitting there a'suckin' of their thumbs with their brains in neutral.'

YORKSHIREMAN, contemptuously surveying the loose weave of a cloth, 'You could riddle bulldogs through it!'

ELDERLY countrywoman, after a night of gales, 'I never knew the wind so vivid, it was past all conscientions.'

AN OLD Norfolk joiner made a book-case, but when put into place against the wall it was out of line. Scratching his head he said, 'Dammet, it be slanting-dicular'.

GLEN shepherd, describing the new laird: 'Och, he's a wee cratur in a deer-stalker, jist like a moose keekin' oot ablow a bushel'.

CORNISHMAN, of offended neighbour: 'Aw, e've gone off with 'is 'air in a knot'.

DEVON woman, describing isolated part of the country where her daughter has gone to live: ''Tes right in the middle of out-the-way-round'.

OLD Sandy, sleeping apart from his wife owing to illness, asked if he had had a good night: 'Nae bad, doctor, but Ah aye sleep best wi' the auld hen in ma oxter'.

The Mobile Society   **Cartoons by Brian Walker**

PERTH woman, of another given to boasting: 'Ay, all her eggs are double yolkit'.

THROUGH TRAFFIC. 'Our Bob said 'e 'ad something in 'is ear. I arst 'im which ear. Then I made 'im lie down an' poured in a little warm oil, an' the earwig come out the other ear'.

THE Parochial Church Council in my Wiltshire village decided to make a charge for rubbing the two brass figures in the church and so the Vicar put a notice in the porch. A female parishioner, reading the notice, stopped the church-warden and remarked: 'Do you see what the Vicar is doing now? He's charging 25p to clean the brass. I think he ought to pay people, not charge them.'

VILLAGE CHORISTER: 'I binna very good at sight-readin', specially them runs. I sees the note a-comin', but afore I can get 'im 'e's gone by'.

NORTHANTS woman, of elderly bachelor: 'Why, if you was ter mention a woman to 'im, 'e'd fly at yer like a bottle o' pop'.

THRESHER, struggling with short loose straw: 'I 'opes before I 'as to 'andle any more o' this 'ere ol' loose trade, I'll be treadin' on me whiskers'.

WARWICKSHIRE groom, hearing distant shout, to his mistress in garden: 'I 'eared the maister 'ooting at you, mum'.

DEVONSHIRE man to friend inquiring after his wife: 'Her's better, but her's still as maze as a hare'.

NOTTINGHAMSHIRE forestry worker, commenting on television ballet programme: 'They wus hoppin' about like frogs what's bin trod on'.

SUFFOLK MAN: 'She's a rare nice woman, give you the top brick off of the chimney if you arst her for it'.

Summer

Village Garden Party, by Brian Walker

The Open Road   by Victor Meek

One day in 1922 I decided that, as soon as I had served my time in India with the R.A.F., I would buy a donkey, load it with a tent, small trade articles, a blow-lamp, solder and other tinkering equipment and travel Britain foot-loose and fancy-free. I would get a pedlar's licence, to be all right with the Law. My training as a fitter would serve, though I would have to learn a bit more about soldering. Handy and willing, I would find all doors open to me. I worked out the costs. Forty pounds should cover everything: donkey, tent and equipment. So for the next three years I made an allotment home of ninepence a day.

I came back to England in 1925 and, while on demob leave, called at the local police station. The sergeant was a smart young man, efficient but friendly. He took some particulars of my intentions and then asked, 'Will you be carrying a pack or pushing a tinker's wheel?'

'I'm going to have a donkey,' I told him, feeling a bit self-conscious.

He put down the pencil. 'In that case it's not our cup of tea at all. We issue pedlars' certificates at five bob a go, provided of course our inquiries as to character and so forth are satisfactory. But the Pedlars Act, 1871, deals only with people who travel without horse or other beast bearing or drawing burden, trading on foot, selling goods for immediate delivery or offering for sale skill in handicraft such as tinkering and chair-mending, grinding knives – that sort of thing.'

'What does a donkey make me then, sarge?'

'A hawker, lad. Nothing to do with us. You need a customs and excise licence costing two pounds, and they won't issue one unless you produce a certificate of good character signed by a clergyman and two local residents, or by a justice, or by a local police inspector who knows you. Then you'd need your name on every package of

goods you carried, and you'd have to produce the licence on demand.'
He gave a chuckle and added, 'But if you trade without one we can't
summons you.'

'Why not?'

'Because the Hawkers Act, 1888, happens to be an Excise Act, so
the police can only arrest you.'

I decided to abandon Neddy. 'What if I travel on foot?'

'Then you just need a pedlar's certificate.'

'And you won't arrest me if I leave it at home, I suppose?'

'Not only may but must, lad. The Vagrancy Act, 1824, lays down a
fine of five pounds on the policeman with a soft heart. He must arrest
anyone found offending against the Act, and uncertificated pedlars
are included.'

I walked to the door. It was not as I had dreamed it would be while
in India.

'There's a way round it, lad,' he said. I turned back. I was
beginning to admire him.

'If you don't sell anything, but just offer for sale your skill in
handicraft, you can have your donkey and come under neither Act.'

It was too late. The open road had ceased to beckon. 'No thanks,
sergeant,' I said, 'I don't fancy the idea any more, somehow. I'll try
something else.'

He would have made a good salesman. 'There's exceptions. You
can sell vegetables, fish, fruit, victuals and coal – and books if
authorised in writing by the publishers. Then again there's . . .'

I interrupted him. 'But there's more snags, I'll bet.'

'Well, of course, if you pitch a tent or encamp on the highway,
which includes the footway, you're liable to be knocked off under the
Highways Act, 1835. And don't forget the viz.'

'The viz?'

'Visible means of subsistence, lad. Most of them keep a tanner in
their boot. Then they can sleep out without interference.'

'Vagrancy Act?' I suggested.

'That's right. Section 4. You're getting the idea.'

I made up my mind. 'Can I have one of those leaflets, sarge?' I
asked, pointing to the desk.

'Now you're talking, lad,' he said with enthusiasm; 'that's more like a job. All the walking you could wish for.'

I sent in my application to join the police that night, and served my time for a pension.

Fiat Justitia   **by L. G. Willcocks**

When holidaying in Westmeath I frequently cycled into the little market town of Ballymote, a pleasant five miles across the bog. On this Thursday morning there seemed to be more activity than usual in the town's one long main street and, meeting Tom Farrell, I inquired the reason. 'Sure,' said Tom, a tall burly R.I.C. pensioner, with a twinkle in his eye, 'it's our monthly petty sessions. Why not come into the court house with me for an hour's free entertainment, if ye've nothing better to do?'

There was just space enough for us on the public benches in the long gloomy court room. The dock was let down about four feet into the floor, behind a rail crowned with a row of long iron spikes. The district justice, a local solicitor, was a small stout ruddy-faced man in plus-fours. 'Got the job because he has the Gaelic speech,' whispered Tom in my ear.

'Call the first case, please,' the clerk instructed the usher, who reeled off some half dozen names at top speed. Several young men and youths filed noisily into the court and clattered down the steps into the dock, where just their heads and shoulders – of the smallest only the head – were visible behind the spiked rail.

'Each of you is charged with cycling on the Dublin Pike at 11.30 p.m. on the night of the twenty-first day of June last, without front or rear lights,' said the clerk. 'Do you plead guilty or not guilty?'

'Guilty, sir,' replied the prisoners with one voice.

'Pay a shilling fine apiece, and next time it'll be half a crown,' said the quick dispenser of justice on the bench. 'Next case, please.'

'Call Thaddeus O'Toole.'

An old man dressed in his best black cutaway coat and striped trousers, with elastic-sided boots and a stiff shirt-front, now entered the dock.

'This charge,' announced the clerk, 'is brought under the Cruelty to Animals section, to wit, working an ass unshod. Call Guard Toomey'.

Guard Toomey stated that he saw the accused drawing turf from the bog on the twenty-eighth of last month, using an unshod ass to draw his cart.

'What have ye to say in answer to this charge?' the justice asked.

'Well, yer honour,' said Thaddeus, 'this is how it is. There is only soft dirt tracks from my old cabin to the bog below, no flint roads at

'Working an ass unshod'

all. I had nothin' on me own feet, an' I see no harm in the old ass workin' the same way as meself.' A roar of laughter from the public benches greeted this reply and was quickly silenced by the usher.

'How old are ye, Thaddy?' inquired the justice.

'Eighty-eight last March, yer honour.'

Justice and clerk held a whispered consultation. Defendant was discharged under the First Offenders Act, and that concluded the cases brought by the Civic Guards.

'Well, Sergeant,' said the justice to the senior policeman in court, 'congratulations on a relatively crime-free month in this most admirable township. We will now proceed with the civil actions.'

'Hannah Doyle against Michael Byrne,' called the clerk.

The use of the dock was now discontinued, and the parties to the action occupied two small witness-boxes placed on opposite sides of the court. A solicitor rose from counsel's benches: 'The plaintiff Hannah Doyle, a widow, claims the sum of £15 for injury sustained by a cow belonging to her, and £5 for loss of a calf. I appear on behalf of the said Hannah Doyle, who will testify that the defendant Byrne beat her cow in a brutal manner with a blackthorn stick, thus causing the said cow to drop prematurely a dead calf.'

Another solicitor rose and informed the court that he represented the defendant, who emphatically denied that he was responsible in any way for the widow's misfortune.

Mrs Doyle, a small thin timid woman who spoke in a voice scarcely above a whisper and frequently had to be told, 'Speak up, please, ma'am' by the justice, said that she heard a disturbance in the field behind her house on May 13. On running out she saw Byrne furiously beating her cow Daisy with a thick blackthorn stick, with the result that the said cow dropped a dead calf the same night.

Defendant's counsel rose to cross-examine: 'Now, Mrs Doyle, please tell his honour where this incident actually occurred.'

'At the gap in the hedge between my field and Byrne's garden.'

'Ah,' said counsel, 'so there is a gap in the hedge. I put it to you that your cow is deliberately encouraged by you to go through this gap to trample, eat and destroy my client's vegetables.'

'Oh, my lord, my lord,' cried Mrs Doyle turning to the justice, 'all wicked lies, all wicked lies.'

'To trample, eat and destroy'

'Liar yerself, ye ould rip', bawled Byrne, breaking his silence and shaking his fist at Mrs Doyle. 'Sure everyone knows it was the wireless that made yer ould cow lose her calf.'

'Keep quiet, Byrne,' said the justice, 'your turn to speak will come. What's all this about wireless? Are ye suggesting, by any chance, that Mrs Doyle's cow was electrocuted?'

Byrne's counsel apologised to the justice for his client's interruption and said that he would produce evidence to the effect that Daisy had been seen with her horns 'tangling' with the wires surrounding the supports of the large wireless aerials of the Athlone

Broadcasting Station, situated at Moydrum and adjoining Mrs Doyle's field.

'Moydrum, did you say?' said the justice. 'Is that where this terrible affair happened?'

'It did, sir.'

'Then please, Mr Clerk, hand me the map, for I am thinking that this case should not have been brought to this court at all, but to the sessions in Athlone . . . Yes, gentlemen,' he announced with a twinkle to both solicitors, after consulting the map of the district, 'you are suing in the wrong district court. You must resolve your dispute elsewhere.' Then to his clerk in a stage whisper, 'And it's not sorry I am that not me but someone else will have to give judgement on that one.'

Drawings by Raymond Piper

A Feud on the Farm   by F. F. Nicholls

Arthur the wagoner and Bert the cowman were mates of mine some years ago on a large arable farm in Kent. Arthur had the traditional appearance of his trade: he was in his late sixties with rich red-brown face, large spreading tobacco-stained moustache and a slow strength which still enabled him to walk about with a $2\frac{1}{2}$-cwt sack of tick-beans on his back. He shared my grandfather's view that a good joke was a good joke for all time; thus he never heard a gun go off without remarking, ''Nother empty bar'l an' Oi ain' 'ad a drop'. He was a cheerful and confirmed atheist – an attitude which, in my experience, is surprisingly widespread among countrymen.

There was nothing whatever traditional about Bert's appearance. Though employed on a farm, he saw no more of the outside air than most factory workers; consequently he was sickly pale, and when he lifted the front of his flat cap his moist brown curls were seen flattened against the damp white skin. Yet he too was massively strong: he used to walk a large Shorthorn bull about like a poodle and carry a four-bushel sack of tail corn like a brief-case. He was a voluble teller of stories, all unprintable and nearly all about 'bits er sport' with girls at the Dreamland amusement park 'down Margit there'. Another favoured topic was his eccentric diet. 'Oi're a queer chap about moi grub, Fred', he would say. 'Milk, milk, milk, all day in 'ere. When Oi git up 'ome Oi carn' stand the soight of it. Never 'ave n' butter on me bread, y'know. Jist a bit er jam, paste, all such as that.'

After I had been at the farm three weeks, the wagoner and I had taken our carts to the cowshed and were helping Bert to muck out. This was unusual, as Arthur was generally carting wurzels at that time of day. We went on working in utter silence, but that was quite normal on any farm; it was not until we had finished that Arthur spoke to me: 'Fred, ast 'im 'ow much straw 'e wants'.

I was astonished, for the two men were standing not more than eight feet apart. 'How many bundles do you want today, Bert?' I asked, sensing a delicate situation.

'Couple er dozen', said Bert, and stumped away to the dairy.

In the stable three hours later Arthur offered an explanation. 'Ole Bert's a funny chap, y'know', he began, seating himself stiffly on the corn-bin. 'You 'ave to goo careful with 'im. Oi carn' make nothing of 'im meself. What! Oi could tell you a few things, on'y it ain' none o'

'There was nothing whatever traditional about Bert's appearance'

moi business.' He paused, wondering which of the few things to tell me first. 'You know th'other day 'e took a bag o' tail corn over for 'is fowls? 'E wouldn't let you take it in the cart next day, same as you offered, would 'e? Well, did you know the ole chap' (the farmer) 'was down town then? Oi ain' saying nothing, moind.' Another pause for thought. ''Nother thing: you know them 'utches where 'e gives out 'e's keeping rabbits?'

I said I did.

'Ferrets! Three-four of 'em. Out with 'em 'e is, pri-noigh every noight. You know Oi went acrost to Fettling Tuesday? Well, as Oi come back past the Wents, there 'e was with a pocketful o' rabbits. 'E went down quick in the doike, but Oi seen 'im alroight. Course, Oi don' say nothing. You know what, Fred? Pri-near makes me croy, the way 'e takes the ole chap in: yes sir, no sir, to 'is face; then setting in that ole dairy rolling fags couple of hours a day an' putting in for everlasting of overtoime. You know that cow what went to the knacker's last week? All 'is fault, y'know. 'E made out there wadn' nothing wrong with 'er, till she doied. Then 'e up an' said 'twas the dusty 'ay Oi took acrost. No, Fred, 'e's a queer feller, an' Oi don' 'ave much to do with 'im. We don' know by roights where 'e come from, y'know. Down Margit way, 'e makes out, but Oi never 'eard of anyone what knew 'im out there. 'Owsumdever, there 'tis; you git some queer old turn-outs these days.'

As far as I was concerned Bert was friendly, cheerful and obliging. When we had finished in the cowshed of a morning he would usually squat back against a wall, as I have seen miners do, saying, 'Well, 'ave a bit er shag now', and pulling out a tin and a packet of papers. Very often this little spell would be filled with unlikely adventures at Margate, but one day I managed to turn the conversation to the subject of Arthur and his family.

'Now there's a mean blooming crowd for you, Fred. Toight as a duck, they are, an' that's watertoight. Whoi, ole Arthur owes me pri-noigh seven-an'-six since last Christmas.'

'Perhaps there's some mistake?'

'Mistake? Ain' no blooming mistake about that, moi Fred. Jis' plain thieving, that's all. Oi give 'im ten bob of a Froiday to git me a 'alf-dollar postal order down town. 'E sent one of 'Orry's little ole boys acrost with it, an' Oi ain' seen moi blooming change yet, an' Oi lay Oi never shall now.'

'Have you ever asked him for it? He might easily have forgotten.'

A bitter snort: 'Oi ain' going to ast 'im for the blooming money; whoi don' 'e come acrost 'ere an' give it me? Oi don' want no favours off of 'im, nit no charity. Course, y'know,' he went on, 'Oi ver-soon

'Arthur spoke to me: "Fred, ast 'im 'ow much straw 'e wants" '

found 'im out, soon as Oi come 'ere from Margit: me an' 'im bought a cant er wood together in that ole shaw 'soide moi 'ouse. Share an' share aloike, supposed to be. Silly-loike, Oi thought Oi'd 'ave enough foiring for all winter out er that. Well, you know what, Fred? Oi lay Oi never 'ad more'n a quarter er that wood. Noight after noight when Oi was in 'er milking, moi ole gal seen 'im goo by with a gurt ole faggot on 'is back. Oi never bought n'more wood along of 'im'.

On another day the subject of straw led us to more of Arthur's failings. 'Well, Fred, Oi carn' 'elp about your raking, Oi shall 'ave to 'ave some more bundles acrost. Oi ain' got nowheres near enough as 'tis. Course, Oi don' say nothing, 'cause about you working with Arthur, but if we 'ad a couple er proper carts coming acrost with it, 'stead er that titchy ole thing 'e roides about on . . . What, Fred! Oi could git as much on the end er moi finger as what 'e gits in that cart. Oi lay when you first come 'ere, 'e never give you the pick er them carts, did 'e? An' that 'orse of 'is ain' on'y 'alf the age er yourn, y'know. Course, it ain' nothing to do with me.' Then with another burst of indignation: 'See, same as when you goo dung-cart, Fred, 'e ain' on'y got 'alf the load to what you got, to chuck up an' rake off, an' Oi lay 'e don' git done any quicker'n what you do. See Fred, 'e's 'aving you all ways. Oh, 'e's clever alroight: toidy soight cleverer'n what Oi are'.

In the eight months that I knew them Arthur and Bert exchanged not a single word. The original quite small but real grievance between them had been built into a great thorny barrier of personal scorn and bitterness. The feud had in fact become a kind of family possession, a thing with a life of its own, which made a good sharp gritty corner in uneventful lives.

Drawings by George Adamson

A Miscellany of Misfits   by Vivian Hill

Working foreman, farm assistant, would-be herdsman – I had them all, from the old muck-and-mystery-been-farming-all-my-life boys to the young men from farm institutes who, after a year's 'practical', felt that farming owed them jobs as herdsmen on generous terms. Of course, there were many in neither category and, luckily for me and the farm, some outstanding chaps among them. I am not writing of these, but of a factual majority none the less.

First came a young couple from a town. Bert donned white overalls and milking cap on arrival and seldom took them off, unless he was dung carting or hauling hay; even then he stuck to his white cap. He was certainly keen and knew all the answers, sometimes anticipating the questions. Not only could he talk about cows and any aspect of farming, but he was evidently widely informed on many subjects, especially literature, sport and, above all, politics: a human encyclopaedia with a mind like a vacuum cleaner. As time went on it became all too clear that his knowledge of dairy cows was more theoretical than practical.

Bert's place and cottage were taken by an elderly farmer and his wife. At least that was the idea, for my advertisement asked clearly for a herdsman; but Okey was an old-timer, scornful of milking machines, milk recording and modern hygiene, and obviously unhappy in the dairy. The farm was a small one and, because the old man was a good all-round stockman and tireless worker, I decided to run it with him as working foreman, and a single young man as assistant potential herdsman. Each aspirant was painstakingly hand-picked on his reply, experience and references. The first came, did an uneasy day's work and retired to bed for a week with a severe cold. The local doctor said he had a weak chest and recommended a move to a drier district.

I next engaged a really proficient young herdsman and congratulated myself on having solved the problem. After two months he announced he was getting married and had a first-class job awaiting him. Perhaps a good girl was the answer. I contacted various bodies, saying I urgently needed a steady girl, thoroughly experienced in milking and dairy work. The bodies were not very hopeful, and I thought no more of it. I simply drafted another advertisement, which produced, among others, Ken, a lean, sallow young gentleman who assured me earnestly that he could milk and was especially keen on dairying. I suggested tactfully that he might be happier elsewhere; but he wrote such a persuasive letter that I relented.

Ken knew how to hand-milk and thought the machine rather funny. In fact, he seemed to find most farm work either an easy-going joke or a stimulant for his health, which was certainly not all it should have been. On several occasions a violent headache obliged him to leave the cowstalls in mid-milking and cycle two miles for a pint of beer 'to buck him up', poor chap. He went off on his rickety bicycle one evening, and we never saw him again.

Sue appeared one morning at breakfast-time, struggling with several suitcases. She had been projected out of the Agricultural Committee's van, which had made off before I could reach the door. 'I'm the land girl', announced Sue breathlessly – evidently the belated answer to my inquiries some months earlier. I thought quickly and, leaving my wife to put the girl at ease, went to persuade Mrs Okey to give her house-room. Until I could convince the lady that Sue's sudden appearance was my surprise no less than hers, I feared she would have hysterics.

'Never been used to this, sir. Not five minutes' notice either. Well, I don't know I'm sure . . .' But at last she relented enough to 'give it a try', and I returned with the glad news. My wife had elicited from Sue that she had had six weeks' training, did not think she liked cows

much and had left her London home 'to get away from Mum and Dad'. After a very dry telephone conversation with an official of the Committee I, like Mrs Okey, finally agreed to 'give it a try'.

Sue did her best, spending hours in the dairy, scrubbing and washing and polishing the machine and utensils; but she never overcame her fear of cows, nor her aversion from muck and mud. The farm was on clay, and the poor girl seemed to get stuck fast in it quite easily, when she would wring her hands and wait for someone to come to the rescue. However, she was soon rescued finally from her unhappy plunge into farm life. She attracted the attentions of a young traveller, a cockney like herself, who took to visiting the farm once a week instead of every quarter. Inevitably Sue soon came to tell me that her young man had got her 'ever such a nice job' in the town.

The Okeys stayed with me for some years. I taught him that machine-milking had advantages other than keeping cigarette ash out of the milk, convinced him of the importance of accuracy in milk recording and checked his tendency to overfeed hay to the cows. I also enlightened him about the prevention and cure of mastitis, which he regarded as a visitation from Above. In return he worked willingly at all hours, always putting the farm and stock before his own interests. So I was sorry when he left on account of his wife's health. It might be wise, I thought, to look for a younger couple.

John and his demure wife took over. Almost at once he brought home to me the fact that a man can farm for some years without being a farmer at heart. He was a strong-looking, upstanding man, and both he and his wife were educated people with urban tastes. He was vocal about his dependence on 'The Times' and keen on classical music and politics. Unfortunately he was less enthusiastic about farm work, which he performed with detached regularity; his cottage door shut at five o'clock precisely. The monotony of various chores I generally had to do later was pleasantly eased by the sound of a Beethoven symphony wafting from John's sitting-room across the wet and windy yard.

One afternoon I was visited by a C.I.D. officer who asked if John was in my employ. I began to wonder if the farm had some fatal attraction for doubtful characters or semi-invalids. John, it seemed, had Communist affiliations. My visitor assured me that nothing

serious was held against him; they just liked to keep track of such people. I was not wholly reassured but did not allow myself to be influenced by this revelation. I observed a few odd-looking visitors calling at the cottage, and that John periodically wore an air of abstracted preoccupation. It was midway through a busy haymaking that he decided to leave. 'Fearfully sorry, but I have obtained a change of occupation'. The following week he was collected by a burly blackcoated fellow and driven away in a large car.

I had not been wholly unprepared for John's sudden departure, and his successors were on the scene within a week. In the Bartlett family it seemed as if at last I might have the real answer to what I was reluctantly coming to recognise as a labour problem: father and mother with an extremely well-developed son of sixteen, ex-farmers, real country stock. It was soon obvious that Mrs Bartlett held the family together, bearing the burden of a testy husband, and tactfully controlling the ebullience of an only son. Young Jim was a good-natured lad and showed the beginnings of a lively interest in modern dairying methods. He was much quicker in the uptake than dad and soon became quite proficient in machine-milking. Nothing I said would induce them to dispense with milking stools for their ample backsides, and this lent a ponderous, clumsy air to the whole operation.

The father proved to be quite uninterested in the quality of the cows, their milk yields and their welfare; he was quick to pooh-pooh any new idea which young Jim might have acquired from reading or even from me. Any undue exertion was likely to aggravate a complaint which required his retirement from work for a day or two. All things considered, I decided to get Bartlett out of the cowstalls and, with optimism only a little dimmed, I once more sent out the kind of advertisement at which I was becoming a master: 'Single young man – live as family – fully expd machine-milking – prospects charge high-yielding herd . . .' This produced Reg, a pleasant young fellow of great character, keen, willing and anxious to learn. Excellent! The only snag was that he intended to get married in a few months and would then need a cottage. The farm had but one, occupied by the Bartletts.

It would be nice to record that all came right in the end. Perhaps in a way it did, for I sold the farm and lived happily ever afterwards.

Drawings by Brian Walker

Mothballs   **by Meston Batchelor**

One half-holiday afternoon of my schooldays I shall never forget, for on it I first met Mothballs. I was cycling across a park to explore its wealth of birds, plants and insects, when I spotted an ancient bicycle leaning against the oak paling that bordered the path. Even in those days it was rare to find a mounting-step projecting from the rear hub: still more unusual were the fixed pedals, thick heavy frame, unsprung saddle and rusty acetylene lamp. But my youthful curiosity was chiefly roused by a bag made of sacking which filled the triangular space under the cross-bar. Not only was it bulging with mysterious shapes, but I could have sworn that I saw one corner give a series of convulsive jerks.

I grounded my own machine and walked hesitatingly across to investigate. At the sound of a rustle in the bracken behind me I turned guiltily; and out of the undergrowth, like a genie rising from a bottle, there gradually emerged a figure so wildly inappropriate to a hot summer afternoon in the country that I stood, my prying fingers still resting on the sacking, rooted to the spot. First a narrow bowler hat with high crown and curly brim appeared, poised disproportionately on an almost circular expanse of bushy black hair. Then came the upper half of an antique morning-coat, green with age, whose open front revealed a stiff white dicky and a waistcoat bisected by a massive silver watch-chain.

Rallying slightly, I withdrew from his bicycle and ventured on a nervous 'Good afternoon'. At the same moment my eye fell on a tangle of bodies squirming energetically between the fingers of his right hand. Without a word he held out two large grass-snakes for inspection.

'Er . . . lovely', I said, feeling awkward. 'How did you find them?'

'I smell 'em', he replied solemnly, and thrust them deep into the sacking. Then, snapping a pair of brown clips round the dark pin-stripe trousers which had now come into view, he hoisted himself up by the mounting-step to the saddle of his venerable machine. I was already sufficiently bewildered but, as he passed me, he burst into an oracular utterance that startled me even more: 'Now the serpent was more sub-til than any beast of the field'. And off he rode at a furious pace, his elastic-sided boots whizzing madly round on the pedals.

My next encounter was equally dramatic. Weeks later I was

Songs Without Words by Brian Walker

spending a half-holiday in the same stretch of country. I had just
flushed a nightingale from an overgrown hazel copse and was peering
inexpertly into the dead leaves for a nest. Suddenly a booming voice
straightened me up with a jerk:

Thou wast not born for death, immortal bird!
No hungry generations tread thee down.

There was the Chaplinesque figure, smiling politely and pointing
only a few feet off to the nest with its five brown eggs.

After this I determined to arrange more meetings; and I soon
discovered that no secret of that countryside was hidden from him.
The birds' nests, the flowering seasons of the plants, the haunts of
butterflies and moths and other insects, badgers' and foxes' earths,
the slots of the roe deer and the dark corners of woods where fungi
flourished in autumn: he knew every one and, seeing that I was
genuinely interested, showed them to me with an eagerness that
matched my own.

Yet at first there were drawbacks to our expeditions. Almost his
only conversation, apart from the name of a specimen or a brief
exclamation to attract my attention, was this unpredictable eruption
of quotations which burst from him like lava from a volcano.
Shakespeare, Spenser and the Old Testament were, I think, his
specialities: but in those days many of them were beyond my range.
Certainly the width of his reading must have been immense. Often,
as we were riding along, the deep bass would boom abruptly out of a
long silence and nearly knock me off my bicycle:

Strew me the ground with daffadowndillies,
And cowslips, and kingcups, and loved lilies:

that was a great favourite of his and would often echo through the
woods on an early spring day. Then there was 'Hark, hark! the lark
at heaven's gate sings', which startled a farmer nearly out of his
senses in one of his own fields. Some bit of information might suggest
a familiar passage, and off he would go. One day he was pointing out
the nest of a sparrowhawk. 'Up there,' he said, 'in that oak — "The
builder Oake, sole king of forests all" — probably four eggs by now'.

When he had had enough he would dismiss me with the phrase,
'Ther' 'tis'; and I went.

By degrees I managed to melt his reserve; and at last a red-letter
day arrived when he invited me to his home. I knew he lived over the
village cycle-shop which he was supposed to run. But alas for the
customers! If the day was fine or some rarity awaited his inspection,
the door, I gathered, was locked, repairs were abandoned and
punctures remained unpatched. I was prepared therefore for the
broken bicycle chains, dirty oil-cans and disintegrating machinery
that greeted me as I crossed the threshold; but not for what I found
when I had followed him up the rickety steps to the two upstair
rooms.

My first impression was of the thick smell of camphor permeating
everything, including the owner. Mothballs, I said to myself. As I
bent my head to avoid the five-foot lintel, stack upon stack of rough
wooden storeboxes, shoulder high against the opposite wall, met my
view. On the left, under a window festooned with cobwebs, stretched
a long deal table almost entirely covered with tightly lidded jars and
glass-topped pill-boxes. At one end was a green baize cloth concealing
a bulky shape I could not at first recognise; at the other a space had
been cleared for a large rectangular vivarium. Here I was delighted

to see the grass-snakes to whose squirmings I owed my first introduction to Mothballs. Everywhere else there were books, on botany, zoology, ornithology, entomology; no branch of natural history was missing nor, of course, the well-thumbed authors whose flowers he plucked so freely. Rising above them to the ceiling were tiers of shelves stuffed with exercise-books containing, so I later discovered, the personal observations of a lifetime.

As I stood contemplating this astonishing Aladdin's cave, the sepulchral voice broke in:

In Nature's infinite book of secrecy
A little I can read;

and, moving over to the table, he whipped off the green baize cloth with a conjuror's flourish to reveal a magnificent microscope, whose value even then must have run into several hundreds of pounds. That was to be the finale of my first visit. He drew a heavy metal watch from his waistcoat and fixed me with a firmly dismissive eye. 'Ther' 'tis', he said.

Happily there were to be many such afternoons. I gradually explored his treasures: collections not only of butterflies and moths but of the more obscure families of insects, fungi pickled in jars, tiny water-creatures in miniature aquaria, mounted slides of plant-sections for the microscope. The variety seemed infinite. Nor shall I forget the enchanted hours spent with the microscope itself. Much later, with almost girlish shyness, he took down some of his exercise-books and allowed me to read the notes he had compiled in his laborious copperplate hand. Hidden in them was a mass of meticulous records which would have been invaluable for any country history.

Gradually too I collected some meagre facts about Mothballs himself. The microscope had been presented by an eminent naturalist for his labours on mycetozoa – tiny fungi whose life-history, he said, had still not been completely worked out. It was, I understood, in lieu of payment offered and indignantly refused. I never found out what he lived on, still less how he afforded his books. I never saw him eat. Of his family I discovered exactly nothing: he had just appeared in

the village from, it was said, the West Country and scratched a living out of his half-derelict cycle-shop.

Then my time came to leave school; and the rest of the Mothballs story reached me only from hearsay, embellished no doubt and possibly even apocryphal. At least it was strictly in character. He was given, so I was told, the job of curator in the school museum, largely to reorganise some collections badly in need of reform. At first all went well, as long as he was left alone with the specimens he loved. The trouble started when visitors approached. He either remained silent or burst out into one of his devastating quotations. His fate was already in the balance with the authorities when a minor royalty, inspecting the school, arrived at the museum just as its curator was deep in a particularly tricky bit of identification and disinclined for interruption. The distinguished visitor bent down to show a genial interest in the operation, but started violently back when a voice as of an Old Testament prophet pealed up at him from a mass of black hair:

O put not your trust in princes, nor in any child
of man: for there is no help in them.

This was the last straw; and the museum saw Mothballs no more.

Some time after I had left, I reflected belatedly, as I fear one does at that age, how much I owed to him, and wrote several times for news; but there was no reply. It was not till years later that I revisited the village. The cycle-shop had disappeared and a garage stood on its site. Of Mothballs the only information I could glean was that he had long ago left the village and was believed to have died in hospital. Of that priceless treasure-house of knowledge not a trace remained.

Drawings by George Adamson

Our House-painting Year   by D. Valley

Having a town house painted is merely a passing chore. Here in the deep South West it is the event of the year – or rather the decade. In April I approach Mr Bricks the local builder and ask for an estimate.

To mark the importance of this ten-yearly occasion, Mr Bricks comes down after tea unrecognisably spruced up in his best suit. We walk slowly round the house ostensibly counting windows but actually looking to see what repairs are inevitable. I have to take his word for it if something on the roof, three storeys up, has to be mended, and I know I can because he is far too kind-hearted to say bluntly that we need a new roof. Instead he will sigh deeply and then cheerfully allow that a nail here and a bit of cement there ought to hold it up for another year or two. And he is usually right.

The final question is when will he start? 'I got to finish Mrs Adam's porch and then do the outside of the club – the inside can be done any time – say Monday week. The actual painting shouldn't take more than four weeks – if the weather's right.'

Monday week I rise early to open the back door so that the men can bring their gear into the workroom. Nobody comes. Each succeeding morning I crawl out early and no one appears. On Friday I wake to slight drizzle. They would hardly start on Friday anyway so I go to sleep again. An hour later I go down to be greeted by cheerful chatter from the back workroom. The men are there and of course, having known this place since they came picking conkers as schoolboys, they know better than I how to twiddle the window latch and climb in.

Tom, Dick and Harry are there, and also, alas, Willy. Willy was only an apprentice last time the house was painted and though his shoulders have broadened and his voice got louder we fear his wit has, if anything, decreased. There is also a small hairy creature, presumably male and presumably the current apprentice. I dare not ask his name outright because he is bound to be the son of someone I know and will be mortally offended that I do not recognise him. After some cautious detective work the apprentice turns out to be Benny the milkman's nephew whom I could not be expected to know. Tom has brought a photo he took last time they painted the house and Dick is full of the new ladder they are having for the high roof. At this bit of news I am torn between alarm at what a new ladder might do to our bill and relief that they have at last abandoned the contraption of three ladders tied with old stockings that they used to mend some slates last winter.

After several cups of tea they disappeared down the drive to paint the lodge. Later I walked down to see how they were getting on. Willy was the only one in sight and he appeared to have at last gone right off his head. He was leaping up and down in front of the parlour window yelling and making fearful faces. When he saw me he stopped but looked quite unembarrassed. 'Er – where are the others?' I asked. 'They'm painting the back. The people went out and left the windows so we can open 'em for the sashes but their dog's loose inside and keeps nipping our fingers. So I 'as to keep 'im mad at the front while they do the back.'

Four weeks Mr Bricks said it would take, but of course that is if nothing happens.

For instance Great Uncle James came to stay and he cannot stand the smell of paint. We explained this and Tom was not the least put out. 'We'll do the backside while he's here. Poor old gent, mustn't spoil his holiday.' And with great goodwill they moved all their ladders round to the back, thereby making double work for themselves. Then there was the morning when they were all

Holiday Hazards

by Arnold Wiles

'I write to draw your attention to . . .'

'Well, if it makes you feel safer'

'It seemed such a nice quiet spot'

splashing gloss paint on the gutters when the fire alarm sounded. Tom, Dick and Harry are the mainstay of the local brigade. We watched with sentimental admiration their incredible speed as they slid down and leapt into the lorry all in one flashing movement and disappeared in a cloud of dust to answer the call of duty. Our admiration dimmed a little when we realised we were reduced to Willy, whose total contribution to the excitement was putting his foot through a pane of glass which then took him all day to mend.

When the firemen returned we took the opportunity to remind them how once they had had a fire practice here and had cleaned our upstairs windows for us with their hoses. 'Couldn't do that now. Our new hoses would blow all your glass in.'

'I suppose, if I gave you some window cleaner and rags, you couldn't give the top windows a rub while you're up there?'

Tom eyed me with a wicked look. He knows quite well that as our windows are all three-sided bows with only the fronts opening it is impossible to clean them from the inside. 'Tell you what, you give us a cup of tea in the afternoon and we'll do your windows.' I say that is blackmail and ask what he would do if I told Mr Bricks. Tom grins happily. 'Well you could tell him, but then you might find all your top window panes painted over instead of cleaned.'

Gradually they work round the house with a fortnight's break when the whole firm goes on holiday. As it was the one heatwave of the year they all returned completely exhausted and suffering from sunstroke. Willy, in particular, seems to have lost all interest and when he is not planting ladders heavily on our most expensive shrubs he is sitting on the grass nursing the cat.

The moment comes that has been secretly worrying me the whole summer. They have reached the high turret window which is just under a chimney stack full of a very healthy swarm of bees. Tom and Harry start a kind of duet to me on how Willy has the best head for heights. Willy loudly agrees. Tom and Harry assist him to put up the big ladder and then quietly busy themselves at a distance. Though the bees can be seen hurling round the chimney like a cloud of biblical locusts no one mentions them.

My conscience pricks. 'Willy, there are a few bees up there. Hadn't you better borrow my bee veil?' He scorns the veil, clumps up the ladder and starts work. I peer fearfully up but the bees do not seem worried. Willy occasionally swipes at the air but continues. I go indoors thinking all will be well.

Suddenly there is a maniac yell and an appalling clatter. I rush out expecting to find a crumpled body, but instead there is Willy running in circles swearing while the others cling to their ladders hysterical with laughter. Although it was only two bees actually inside his shirt they caused his downfall I thought gloomily that that was one window that was not going to be done. To my amazement Willy, having finally found the bees and destroyed them, put on the bee veil and went straight up the ladder again and finished the job.

As they collected their ladders to leave at the end of July, I calculated how long the estimated four weeks had stretched. Over three months! Then I looked in my diary and counted the actual days they had been painting, and found they amounted to exactly twenty-eight days. I should have trusted Mr Bricks. Four weeks he said and four weeks it was.

A Kiss from a Cow   by Hartley M. Jenkinson

On our station near Masterton in North Island, New Zealand, in 1905, we had an Ayrshire cow called Betsy — so named because she looked like an aunt of ours. We reared her from birth when her mother died and taught her many tricks; to offer a foot to shake, to take salt from our hands when we said 'Salt, Betsy', and even to 'kiss'. In time she could do this perfectly with no slobber, just the 'whiskery' touch one gets from an aunt well 'on the shelf '.

'Why not?' asked Dad, to our enquiry about putting Betsy in the next show. 'But you'll have to do all the work.' At the judging our faces shone nearly as brightly as Betsy's coat. The day was hot, with no wind. We sweltered and so did the judge, Mr Saltbridge. He looked hard at the three other entries in our class, then came back again to Betsy. When he placed his hand on her foreleg, she raised it, as we had taught her, and held it for the judge to shake. He did not, and Betsy was not amused. But Mr Saltbridge next bent down and had a hard look at her face. She stretched out her neck and kissed

Arnold Wiles goes to Church

'That should hold the tower for a while but it's a pity we had to sacrifice the lichgate'

'Bad news, vicar. The bats have deserted the belfry'

him lightly on the cheek. That fixed it; Betsy got first prize! But just then a steward came up and called, 'Mr Saltbridge, Mr Saltbridge, may I see you for a minute?' Betsy waited no longer. She had heard the call 'Salt' twice. Leaning forward she gave the judge the best licking he ever had from a cow.

Another animal we owned at Wairarapa was Napoleon, Dad's pride and joy. As a foal he was not much to look at, all legs and a Roman nose, jet black with a white star. As a three-year old, Nap, as we preferred to call him, was trained as a hunter and won many small steeplechases. We children rode Nap a lot.

About this time the local show instituted a 'Victoria Cross' race in its programme. The horses were in pairs at the starting line. At the word 'Go' the first of each pair would gallop down the course for about half a mile, whereupon the rider pretended to have been shot and fell off. The other one of the pair would then mount, race down the course, halt by his companion, heave him into the saddle, clamber up behind and gallop back to the finish. The winner was the one who brought his man back first. Many a day when Dad was out with the stock on his second horse we were practising the V.C. race with Nap. We could jump off at a gallop, Nap would skid to a halt, help us grab the 'wounded soldier' and gallop home.

But Dad was coaching Nap for the three-mile steeplechase. At the big race Nap looked the best horse there. At first Dad kept him well to the rear of the field and then slowly caught up till they were lying second. A quarter of a mile from home the leading horse fell and threw its rider heavily. Instead of taking the lead Nap promptly skidded to a halt, nearly pitching Dad over his head, and half turned round to shield the fallen rider from the approaching thundering mob of horses. Dad realised that he had now no hope even of a place, so did the next best thing. He slid off Nap to help the casualty. Seeing that no bones were broken he lifted the chap into the saddle, jumped up behind, and made for the first-aid tent. The spectators gave the usual applause to the winner but the ovation Dad got was tremendous. He was reckoned the sportsman of the day.

Mum never told about the training we children had given Nap for the V.C. race. And Dad did win the steeplechase on Nap for the next six years.

The Last Gardener
by R. A. Reeves

Illustrated by Dennis Mallet

Fought Fate, its winds and its weeds,
for eighty years
but finally got carried off
by that ancient enemy of his,
a late April frost.

He won't be missed;
the one true artist in a village
levelled out to bland estates
with flowering shrubs and cocktail talk
and classes in pottery.

Stubborn as bindweed, cunning as ivy,
he picked up some pints
playing rustic to fools
but where his craft was concerned
was not to be moved.

The journeyman of Nature
respected its rules, would ever scorn
the trickster's ways to quick effect,
the skill in his hands
being honest and proud.

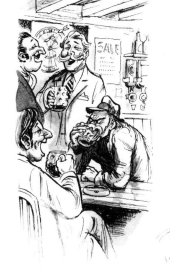

Kept all his life
an eye for beauty: the flame
of a rose in the morning sun,
dragonflies . . . and girls, the marble-sweet limbs
of brief-skirted girls delighted him.

Hates he nourished
fierce and blind: nasturtiums;
women in trousers; posh-talking men;
the fashion for hormones,
– and he couldn't abide cats!

Last of his line he lived to see
the pride of his life's work
bull-dozed for bungalows,
yet never succumbed
to the rust of regret.

Lived like an outlaw,
rough and free, in Woodbine Cottage,
the wreck behind the Natal Clinic:
died quiet as an oak
from a surfeit of time.

Estate Secretary   **by Christine Chapman**

My first introduction to the County Association of Farm Secretaries was on a day course at the Agricultural College. This included an intensive talk on something called 'Cash Flow and Budget Analysis'. After lunch we were set a sort of test : it was rather like doing a geography examination when you cannot remember whether Oslo is the capital of Sweden or Norway, and I gazed in admiration at the pens scribbling away around me. What a learned and intelligent gathering of farm managers and secretaries! The only thing was that none of the things they had been talking about all morning seemed to apply to my estate secretary's job!

Still, I must have learnt something, because next morning I hurtled into His Lordship's office full of enthusiasm for revising the cash books. His Lordship gave me a cool look and remarked that while he was delighted to learn that I wished to improve myself, it might be more to the immediate point if I were first to telephone Daimler Hire for a car to meet him and Her Ladyship in London, whither they intended to travel that day, and second, make an appointment for Her Ladyship to have a facial. Furthermore, I would appear to have been careless in cooking my family's breakfast that morning, since I had a spot of grease on my jumper. As a matter of fact any mention of book-keeping offended His Lordship, and I had to do the books on days when he was out, as the mere sight of the adding machine, which he had been forced by me to buy, and that enormous cash book produced by the National Farmers' Union, sent him up the wall. Not a very promising start!

I resolved to try again with the farm manager, Mr Havant, in the afternoon when he came in for his daily bind. Mr Havant's reaction was different from His Lordship's; for one thing it was very much louder. As far as I recall the gist of it was that it would be more effective if I were to devote my spare time to persuading His Lordship to buy some blasted Friesians, or we would never get the blasted milk output up since he never had any blasted grazing to bring on heifer calves because of the blasted pheasant cover.

In case my readers should have gained the impression that His Lordship was adopting a flippant and unrealistic approach to modern farming, let me hasten to assure them that the farm was very much a going concern, under the capable care of Mr Havant, who daily studied closely the mental and physical needs of every animal. A happier and more contented bunch of cows would have been hard to find, and our milk production compared favourably with the best in the county. Still we were supposed to be increasing the herd, and in due course a score of Friesians arrived. His Lordship regarded these with distaste and remarked that they would look damned unattractive standing in the park and brown and white cows were far more decorative. This sentiment at first shocked us all, but not a week had passed before we were repeating that they did in fact look rather dreary. However, now that we were taking our farming seriously, Mr Havant persuaded His Lordship that all that was still necessary was a Friesian bull.

After a few weeks an animal about the size of an African elephant appeared, by the name of Homer, and massive padlocks were purchased to contain him within his pen. I was not present at his first marriage ceremony, but I gather that the rest of the estate was, from Her Ladyship down to the cowman's youngest child. I learnt that it was all rather a fiasco really as Homer was an ex-artificial insemination bull and could not tell one end of a cow from the other, although he did cast an amorous glance at the cowman. I still wonder how Homer was given the necessary instruction . . . but never asked in case anyone told me the answer.

If there was one thing that really stirred His Lordship it was the mention of seeing snipe in Water Meadow at dawn, or some other feathered species that he could massacre during the only interesting time of the year, the pheasant shooting season. After a very dull morning dealing with letters and being bullied by Mr Havant, sometimes it would turn out to be a good day after all – if the gamekeeper appeared and suitable stands could be discussed for the season.

The gamekeeper, Mr Cushing, closely resembled his charges. In fact it would be hard to find another man whose nose so resembled a beak. He was also the biggest scoundrel in a twenty-mile radius. Luckily for him, his cottage was at the far end of the estate, and the garden was full of scrap, old cars and mysterious sheds full of

Green Fingers   by Arnold Wiles

'It all began with a couple of tubs and a window box'

'Even his bonfires smell sweeter!'

'My husband couldn't grow mustard and cress but he's good at anything mechanical'

'acquired' property, all of which he would stoutly maintain was the property of his sons. Mr Cushing's sons were a deal handsomer than Mr Cushing. One look from their black insolent eyes made one realise that there was little possibility of a decline in the birth rate in the surrounding villages. However, Mr Cushing was the Keeper, and so, in His Lordship's eyes, far less boring than the rest of us.

In the spring Mr Cushing was given 'broody hen money', a sum of about £10 a week to purchase hens. The previous year having thrown some doubt on his ability to calculate correctly, he was instructed to keep a little book so that the purchases could be recorded. This time he was so anxious to avoid such a slur that when I looked at the book I found he had apparently received only about £70 for the purchase of around 300 hens. At the going price of 25s per hen this seemed rather odd. I thought he had rather over-reacted and told him to take his book away and have another think before presenting it to His Lordship. I then rushed home and counted my hens. You cannot be too careful.

All our employees were very tall, although on the neighbouring farm the workers resembled the weatherbeaten rugged short-legged characters of a Peter Breughel painting. I always pondered on the ecological difference. But mentioning tall men reminds me of the Day of the Cesspit.

I was closeted in the sitting room with the accountant when the cesspit man was ushered into the room. He wore a puzzled and defeated air. His problem was that he had been down in the field emptying the pit, gone away to deposit his load, returned to replace the cover on the pit, and to his amazement found it full again. He had repeated this manoeuvre three times and told me he was afraid he might be employed at His Lordship's premises all day unless the entire family stopped having continuous baths immediately. Leaving the accountant, I accompanied the cesspit man into the garden, where we were met by the sudden roar of angry voices followed by the noise of heavy feet pounding across the gravel. For a moment I thought that someone had forgotten to put the padlock on Homer's gate again, but no: it was Mr Havant, with the swimming pool man, who was carrying out his summer servicing of the pool which entailed emptying its contents; and the gardener, Mr Hazel.

Now the story was rather complicated, but evidently the swimming pool man had proceeded, in all innocence, to empty the contents of the swimming pool on to the lawn. Mr Hazel had interceded and told him to stop as last year this procedure had killed Her Ladyship's lawn. He then suggested pumping the water into the cesspit drain: hence the cesspit man's dilemma in the next field. At the time I joined them the water was back-tracking on to the drive and swamping the lawn again. Meanwhile Mr Havant had arrived to protest that the cesspit was overflowing swimming pool water on to his wheat, and moreover, was being sprayed over grazing land, which would kill the grass, etcetera.

The noise was indescribable: all four men followed the customary country procedure of starting to shout when faced with any situation out of the ordinary. What is more, I seemed to be in the middle of the group, and was badly placed if they decided to resort to fisticuffs. Taking a deep breath I fired off a burst from a child's machine gun which happened, by good fortune, to be lying around on the lawn, and called for silence in excellent imitation of my son's schoolmistress. This had an immediate effect. I then delivered a short pithy speech containing entirely useless phrases such as 'use . . . initiative' and 'a solution must be found', and other advice which would be of no assistance at all (I had by that time picked up a thing or two from His Lordship's army stories); and stalked back to the house swinging the gun. A solution was duly found.

It turned out to be a good day for His Lordship. He was so delighted when I told him about the Cesspit Drama that he gave me a large gin-and-tonic.

Refreshing Sight   by J. M. Haggart

While visiting a small West Highland port one summer afternoon I wanted a cup of tea, but could see no sign of a tea room. I therefore approached a youth working nearby and asked him, 'Is there a café about here?' 'Yes there is,' said he. 'Well, if there is I haven't seen it.' 'I'll show you.' He led the way to the byre, opened the door, and there lying on straw in a pen was a small brown and white calf.

Far From the Madding Crowd   **by Dennis Mallet**

Scarecrows I Have Met   **by Dawn MacLeod**

When an old 'tattie bogle' came to light recently at the back of a derelict Cotswold cottage, early memories prompted me to lift the limp muddy relic and take it home. Because the helmet hat was shaped like a topee and coloured a dim khaki, I named the creature General Pukka, though the rest of his attire, consisting solely of what the trade calls gentlemen's long underwear, was hardly in keeping with the dignity of the title. His arms, made from a pair of lightly stuffed cotton stockings, hung loose from beanstick shoulders and flew out in sudden realistic gestures when caught by the wind.

'Ah,' said a neighbour, 'I reckon he's one of Mrs Twinning's; she's a dab hand at making scarecrows. Been at it for years.' This gave me an idea. General Pukka had such a genial personality; why not get a pukka memsahib as companion for him?

Mrs Twinning, alert as a squirrel, was keen to discuss her work as a master scarecrow-builder; but when I gave details of my requirement her face fell. 'A female woman scarecrow? Oh, I don't know about that. I've never made ought but a man. But look, I'll show you the one that goes to church fêtes and flower-shows. He's in the front room if you'll step inside. We take the stuffing out of him and he folds up for the winter; still, you'll get an idea.'

The armchair beside her parlour grate held a woebegone figure in a state of collapse, with tow hair spread limply on the cushions,

boneless trouser-legs folded against his hollow chest, and a pair of bedroom slippers askew on the seat.

'He does look ill', I murmured, startled by the anguished stare of large coat-button eyes in a grey canvas face.

'Oh yes, he is. He always has a pain somewhere, you see, and when he goes to a fête people pay sixpence for a pin-on flag and stick it into him where they think the trouble is. The one who gets nearest the right spot wins a prize. It's a great draw; pounds and pounds he makes for charities. He gets driven all over the county in summer-time, and they even borrowed him down to Wiltshire last August.'

So the scarecrow of today had gone into show business, travelling by car, living soft and lying up during the winter. But I went away from Mrs Twinning's cottage still determined to provide the General with a mate; and the sight of a discarded American fashion-hat in my wardrobe decided me to do the job myself. Originally acquired for a women's literary luncheon in the States, this cute little Fifth Avenue 'whimsy' had not met with esteem from my family; they told me I looked like a scarecrow in it. Why not then use it for a stuffed memsahib? That embroidered muslin dress would do for her too; I had always felt uncomfortably feline beneath its spots. For her head there was the shrimp-pink lampshade brought at a youth club bazaar. The parchment cone was soon painted with sultry eyes and seductive lips and perched on a coat-hanger, from which the dress

swayed in graceful folds, supported by a tripod arrangement of bamboos.

I planted the lady beside her General and was contemplating the happy pair when a whoop from the next-door garden made me jump.

'Coo, look, she's made a girl fer 'im. Look, Bert, she's a smasher!'

'Coo, yes. Let's make a scarecrow too!'

'What, us'n?'

'Coo, yes, a spaceman! One o' they red bottles 'll do fer 'is 'ead. You run an' ask Mum fer an old 'at to put on top.'

The following morning I found a glaring scarlet-faced spaceman in an arrogant stance close to the garden paling, and Memsahib propped limply against the General's chest. The night's gale could have been responsible, but it looked very like shock. At any rate she never fully recovered, and eventually collapsed altogether, leaving no trace – or so I thought, until close examination of a thorn bush showed me the wreckage of my twelve-dollar hat tucked away under the bottom branches. It was spring, and a wren was busy building her nest amid the pink velvet roses and bows, with little scraps of eye-veil neatly woven into the lining. After all, there is nothing like a scarecrow to attract birds.

Drawings by Dawn MacLeod

Summer Tail Corn

A LITTLE measly talk over neighbours is right enough; it do make the day go by a little quicker and sends a body to bed with a chuckle.

FROM the Weald of Kent: 'I'm not goin' down that there ellinge road by the scroopy gate' [*ellinge*, lonely or uncanny; *scroopy*, squeaky].

'AH, she's eighty-seven an' still battin', but she doan't run between t'wickets nah': a Yorkshireman, of course, about his mother.

POSTMAN, when asked why he had changed his political allegiance: 'Ye maun bend tae the buss that bields ye best.' (You must bend to the bush that shelters you best.)

HEARD on a farm: 'Oi told him what he could do with his eggs, an' he reared up loike a bit o' froid bread.'

FYLDE (Lancashire) organist, explaining why he had turned down a better-paid post: 'Ah sin t'organ, an' when Ah tooched t'keyboard, it were like a coople o' skeletons tumlin' down a marble staircase.'

SOMERSET WOMAN, describing a bride at her wedding, ''Er was nervous as a cat, trembling like a leaf and white as a maggot, poor maid.'

FOREST OF DEAN gardener, finding death's-head caterpillar among his potatoes: 'Thic's a queer un, zurree. Thou mind if 'im were about dree vit long I reckon 'im da make tha creep.'

THE LIMPSFIELD MONSTER. A jobbing gardener, asked if he had ever seen an adder in the district, replied: 'Not in Oxted I 'aven't, but in Limpsfield I 'ave. Nine yards long it were. Give my wife a turn it did.'

DAUGHTER of Devonshire farm worker retired from tied cottage to seaside town: ''E doan't like it at all. See, trouble is 'e 'as to wear a collar an' make 'isself a little bit thereafter.'

DAILY HELP, announcing that a neighbour had rats in the house, 'She's not worried, they've already sent for the rotarian.'

SCOTTISH proverb: 'There's aye some watter whaur the stirkie drooned.' (There is always some water where the young bullock drowned – i.e. no smoke without fire.)

OLD HEDGER, knocked over by a charging tup, 'Oh 'twere nothing like, 'e were only playful, not lungerous mind.'

OLD FARMER to his wife, on first seeing the sea, 'Look ee there Martha there be aacres and aacres on it!'

WILD LIFE. An old lady who had seen a cinema show – a natural history picture – said to her companion, 'What kinds of birds were they?' 'I don't really know,' said her friend. 'No, I don't know either: at first I thought they were cuckos but when I saw the eggs I knew they weren't cuckoos because they don't lay their own eggs.'

ENERGY OUTPUT. A Northamptonshire woman said of her husband, who was always wandering off at the start of one job to do something else, 'He's the only man I ever knew who boiled his shaving water three times.'

LINCOLNSHIRE railway porter, when asked the time of the next train: 'Why, there's one at some'at to four, or some'at after four, or some'at.'

OLD YORKSHIREMAN, lifting his face on a warm damp evening to feel the gentle warm rain, 'By gow, but it's a rich neet.'

LANCASHIRE FARMER'S WIFE, calling her sons on a Monday morning, 'Ged up: day after termorrow's Wednesday – then there's nobbut Thursday and Friday and t' week's ower and nowt done.'

OLD MAN in Nottinghamshire called to his wife, 'It's welly ten o'clock an' after. She willunt come now, sure to.'

BERKSHIRE woman after disturbing some wood lice under a stone in the garden, 'Oh, I can't abide they chisel-pigs; they makes I criddle all up.'

YORKSHIREMAN indicating chap in a hurry: 'If he were cawd he'd not hev t'time ter shiver.'

Autumn

Village Fête and Gymkhana, by Thelwell

Trees and Tribulations   **by Jean Davis**

'You wouldn't think,' said the President of the Women's Institute,
'that it would be so difficult to give something away!'

The idea of donating six trees to the village playing field had
seemed so simple and philanthropic and far-sighted – yet it had taken
months to arrange. Democracy being what it is in rural affairs, the
proposal, mooted in the Women's Institute committee, had duly been
brought up at the monthly meeting. The Secretary had then written
to the Clerk of the council, who had laid the matter before the parish
councillors, who had referred it to the Playing Field sub-committee.
Here the Gilbertian element crept in, as this sub-committee
comprised all the parish councillors plus three independent members.
It took a full two hours and five minutes for all the implications to be
discussed, during which time every parish councillor reversed his or
her previously-made decision. However, the motion to accept the
kind offer of the Women's Institute was passed,. by a narrow
majority, with an amendment that the Sports Club should be
consulted as to the siting of the trees.

All possible avenues having been explored constitutionally, they
were retraced, laboriously and painstakingly, to the culmination of a
meeting of all interested parties on site.

The grey drizzle gathered in droplets on bobble hats, deer-stalker
and trilby, head scarves and berets. The Vicar's wife (a parish
councillor) danced gaily in from the swirls of mist, her anorak
sodden; she had the very place.

The Doctor (Playing Field sub-committee) looming up, said 'No'
very firmly and then asked where she had in mind. When told, he
asked how the cutter could get between the trees and the boundary
wall, whether the Parish Council had considered pannage and
herbage, and anyway, triumphantly, surely there was a Bye-Law?

He was supported, unexpectedly, by the Chairman of the Parish Council who also said no, because he was going to have his public convenience and his bus shelter in that space, and the roots would undermine his foundations. The Schoolmaster, the Village Elder and the Vicar's wife (councillors all) pounced in unison.

'What right have you to take decisions on behalf of the whole council?'

'The minute of 21 July states specifically . . .'

'Planning permission . . .'

The Doctor's alsatian and the Schoolmaster's labrador, with a perfect sense of timing, chose this moment to continue their long-standing if desultory feud, and launched themselves across the feet of the dissentient parties. Their owners, with the expertise of long practice, merely slipped their respective leashes and retired two paces. Unfortunately the Chairman of the Parish Council, for a mistaken sense of gallantry, cried for the ladies to fear not, and raised his knobbly ash stick to part the combatants. This had the effect of uniting everyone against him, and long before the hubbub died the two dogs were rabbiting amicably in the outer mist, which had been their intention all along.

The Forestry Officer who had been standing, bewildered, with the moisture trickling between his hat and his collar, volunteered that, if everyone really wanted to know, the statutory distance from a wall was 25 ft; he added, in the digestory pause, that he had marked the holes for the flowering cherries and that young Billy and young Peter were ready to dig. Everyone smiled in a self-congratulatory fashion, a state of euphoria which was only slightly dulled when the Vicar's wife asked brightly whether the trees included any laburnums, as they were frightfully poisonous to the children, did they know? This elicited a frigid reply from the President that considering she (the Vicar's wife) had written three letters on the subject, had lobbied most of the members of her (the President's) committee, and had mentioned the toxicity of these shrubs in at least half a dozen telephone calls, no, there were no laburnums.

The Schoolmaster interrupted to ask whether he was correct in assuming that a copper beech was to be included, because, if so, there would be a problem with regard to root growth. The Chairman of the Sports Club asked who was a-going to sweep up all them leaves, and when asked by the Doctor whether a nice bit of shade would not be welcome over the pavilion, gave a categoric no, and what about leaves bunging up the guttering? The Vicar's wife swept the Forestry Officer into the deepening mist in order to explore the far corner of the field, leaving the Mothers' Union representative to murmur that if the trees were to be secreted in outer space, surely the whole object of the exercise would be defeated?

The Doctor hastily started a gracious little speech – 'Expressing

the feelings of the whole parish — the generosity and far-seeing thoughtfulness . . .' — but the wanderers returned, announcing that they had found the perfect site over the bank, and that the couple in the cottage had no objection. The Chairman pronounced in satisfied tones that that should do it, and a general shifting of thoughts to dry clothing, opening time, and the joint in the oven could be felt.

The Forestry Officer mentioned, diffidently, that the trees would need protection against the sheep, and this brought various representatives into a huddle to find out which organisation could produce the best reasons for not having to provide fencing, wiring and labour, a contest which the Playing Field committee lost.

The Doctor, looking at his watch, continued his speech, to be cut short by the President, who thanked him, said she would inform her members of his kind remarks, and muttered, as she turned away, that you wouldn't think, would you, that it would be so difficult to *give* something away?

Drawings by Brian Chandler

Dressing for the Part   **by Hilary Mason**

I am fairly new to gardening. In fact, remembering Judith Bliss, the actress in Noel Coward's play *Hay Fever* who comes sweeping in remarking grandly that she has been 'pruning the calceolarias', we theatricals are not supposed to know very much about it. Until three years ago my husband and I lived in a sixth-floor flat with nothing more soil-stirring than a window-box to cherish. If someone had asked me then what I should wear if I ever had a real garden to look after, I suppose I should simply have said 'my oldest clothes'.

Now that we live in the depths of the country and I have had to take gardening much more seriously, I find that I do indeed wear old clothes, mostly my husband's, but there is a choice among even these ancient rags, and some are more comfortable and conducive to easy tilling than others.

I was caught in the entire set the other day by a lady who, receiving no reply from knocking on my front door, nipped smartly round to the back and caught me turning out the garden shed.

'I hope you don't mind,' she said, 'but I wanted to ask you to open the Autumn Fair – it's in aid of our church and you actresses always add a bit of glamour.'

I did not blame her for looking at me somewhat doubtfully as she said this – my glamour must have been pretty questionable just then.

I had no make-up on to start with. The slightest perfume from facecream or lipstick seems to drive the wasps and flies into a frenzy, and no amount of hand-flapping and swearing will put them off. Then, my hair was almost entirely hidden under the old rain-hat I was wearing as protection from the cobwebs and other nastiness I was sweeping down with my broom. If I had not been sporting the rain-hat it would have been an ancient straw hat in which my father was wont to go bowling: this keeps the sun out of my eyes and off the back of my neck, and prevents my expensive hair-tint being bleached to a brassy yellow. I have tried other forms of head-gear, being slightly envious of Elizabeth the First's garden hat, which reposes in a glass case at Hatfield House – and a delightful piece of straw nonsense it is too – but then I daresay Elizabeth never had to hoe in a high wind, and what I really need is something I can pull over my ears that stays on!

My legs were clad in a pair of my husband's cast-off trousers, and to top this I had pinched one of his old cotton shirts – nylon does not absorb the sweat which pours off me as I dig, dig, dig. Round my middle I had on my gardening apron, which is useful for popping in the keys to the garden shed, tiny trowel for weeding the lawn, scissors, string, secateurs, and all the hundred-and-one things I leave

lying around and eventually lose. They always turn up again but often rusty and quite unusable. Invaluable indeed is my apron, but it does make me look like a kangaroo with a couple of little ones in my pouch.

My Wellingtons were caked with mud. I have tried wearing shoes, but except on the very hottest days when I have no business to be gardening anyway, Wellingtons keep my feet cool and dry, or warm and dry as the weather may require. I did start off with a pair a size too large, thinking they would be more comfortable to work in; but I used to tramp straight out of them, leaving them behind on flower beds or falling over them. Besides, rubber boots that leave lots of room for your feet also leave lots of room for soil, stones and small insects to get in, and I spent a great deal of time balancing on one boot and shaking out the other.

I also tried doing without gardening gloves, as most of the people in our village do, and certainly when it comes to tying up chrysanthemums or weeding between strawberry plants I prefer plain fingers. But I always regret it and cannot get my nails clean for days afterwards. In fact I often wear two pairs of gloves, an old cotton pair under the toughest gardening ones.

My visitor was not to know this of course, but I am also very choosy as to what I wear underneath my top dressing. I once made the mistake of trying to 'break in' a garment by doing the gardening in it; a lovely thing it was, vastly expensive and with enough uplift and downpull and clinching-in to satisfy the most fashionable taste. However, it certainly was not made for all that bending, lifting, stooping, pulling and other exercises the waist is heir to when gardening, and on disrobing I found my middle was patterned like a waffle iron. Ever since I have worn a really disreputable thing that I think I broke in during the Middle Ages, and tights that are really just holes held together by a nylon strand or two.

I once portayed a lady gardener on the stage: all drifting grey chiffon and high-heeled shoes, trug held delicately in one white hand, secateurs in the other and not so much as a genteel leaf or a spot of sweat to disturb my cool, unruffled appearance. I shall know better next time!

Drawings by Dennis Mallet

Life in a Village

by Brian Walker

As an artist Mr Walker has illustrated *Countryman* articles for many years. He is also a countryman born and bred, chairman of his parish council and deeply immersed in rural life. We asked him this time to comment, in his own style, on village life. But it is not his village or his neighbours; all places and faces are fictitious.

'All things bright and beautiful . . .'

The successful farmer

The bankrupt farmer

Happy farmer going to market

Miserable farmer coming home

Aristocratic farmer

Tenant farmer

WHO LIVES WHERE

Senior advertising executive

County ploughing champion

Managing director

Whipper-in of foxhounds

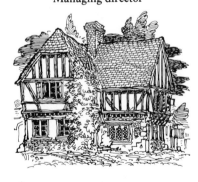

Night-club proprietor

Farrier

'Those new potatoes you gave us were simply gorgeous – how do you manage to get them so tasty?'

PARENT TEACHERS' ASSOCIATION

'Have you washed, combed your hair, cleaned your teeth, been to the toilet, are your shoes clean, have you got clean handkerchiefs?'

'Yes, and be quick about it!'

THE WOMEN'S INSTITUTE

THE CHURCH FETE

'A moveable feast, eh Vicar?'

'Such a change to come to one of these quaint old village inns – so full of local charm . . .'

The man who found the answer to nocturnal car rallies

Good Years for Bad Eggs   by J. W. Smith

It was all over for another year. The crowds had gone, the show benches were cleared and the men came in to take down that giant marquee, the flower-show 'big top', and transport it twenty miles for yet another display of garden produce and village industry.

Once again our show was a great success, but while we were looking over the industrial section we remembered old Emma, who is no longer with us. Now Emma was a brown egg specialist who took the first prize every year. We in the village knew, of course, that Emma's birds were white Leghorns which never laid brown eggs. We also knew that Emma never owned a Welsummer or Rhode Island Red which are regarded as brown egg producers, yet she was able to show year after year a splendid clutch of six evenly matched brown eggs. 'I polish 'em' she told us, but the old boys knew she had used a tan shoe polish, and in generous doses.

Old Emma took first prize year after year. Then an awkward judge decided to break one of the eggs. Emma was unplaced and a vile smell pervaded the marquee to the end of the show. She had shown the same 'brown' eggs for eight years!

Tom John Whittaker, our one-time raspberry expert, also took a first every year until that sad occasion just before the war. It had been a hot summer and the fruit ripened early. Then came the rain, a week of it, and Tom John discovered he was short of raspberries and could not make up the required pint. Like everyone else in the village, Tom John knew that Cuthbert, landlord of the 'Fleece', had a few good canes at the back. He decided to 'borrow' just enough to make up his pint.

The night before the show was black dark, with a drizzling rain. Tom John crept up the snicket at the side of the 'Fleece', made his way quietly over the fence towards the raspberry canes, and found someone else there, apparently bent on the same errand. Tom John flashed his torch: the poacher was the village constable! That year P.C. Hammond took first for raspberries, while Tom John's entry was disqualified for being short measure.

'What about cauliflowers,' asks old Harry Benson at one committee meeting, 'how many entries last year?' 'Well, now, that raises a problem,' replies our secretary. 'Last year we had twenty-six, but it all depends what Polly Allison can get when she takes her van to market. She got a real top-class box on show day last year and the lads were able to pick out some good entries.'

The committee stipulated another year that onion tops should be left on, after Harry recalled that a chap from the town had taken first prize with three massive onions bought from a greengrocer. Harry considered that the 'tops on' ruling would eliminate these 'townees' because shops sell with tops off.

Then there was Granny Errington, who showed her elderberry wine each year with outstanding success. That bottle was brewed when Victoria was on the throne and won first prize for almost forty years. Three generations of Erringtons showed that precious wine until young Iris accidentally dropped the bottle as she was dusting it for yet another show. Each year the bottle had been depleted by the sampling sips taken by the judges, but each year it was topped up with gin!

Brightening the Churchyard   by Margaret Macbrair

Only a newcomer to a village, unaware of the personal feuds and feelings which incapacitate the rest of us from any immediate or decisive action, will take on the chairmanship of a churchyard sub-committee. We found one in a retired army officer. Unlike his fellows in rural fiction, he does not shout at the top of his voice or live genteelly on his pension; he commutes quietly and regularly to the nearest town, where he does a nine-to-five job. He had to leave India when independence arrived, so he went as an administrator to an African colony. When it too gained independence, he came to our village. Here he is determined to stay; no independence for us.

In the spring he organised the farmers with men, tractors and mowers to clean and clip the churchyard. His zeal spread beyond its stone walls, and one evening I found myself collecting litter along the main street with the rector. The result was that we rose from nineteenth to second in our division of the Best Kept Village competition. The parish council were delighted with the parochial church council; their memberships are almost but not quite identical. Some of the local inhabitants wondered what on earth other villages were like, but were on the whole pleased. We all thought we could sit back and rest on our laurels. But the chairman of the parish council sent notes to all village organisations, explaining our position and suggesting that, with suitable effort, we might come first next year. He then left for America and the vice-chairman, who thought any preparation for next June's judging would be unfair, stepped into his shoes. But the chairman of the churchyard sub-committee was keener than ever.

As a member, co-opted while my mind was elsewhere, I had once suggested that flowering shrubs and bulbs would make pleasant additions to the existing lay-out of yew trees and tombstones. The Colonel reminded me of this whenever we met. He embellished my original idea: couldn't I get the Sunday School to do the planting? Then the youth of the village would take a pride in the flowers, which would be protected, not picked. I agreed it was a lovely idea – at a sherry party when autumn was still a long way off. By September, when we sat side by side taking the entrance money at the flower show, he was getting insistent. On the spur of the moment I thought hope might lie in the union of the churches. I promised to ask a Presbyterian neighbour who had a Hebridean bulb farm; and a short time later a bulging sack of daffodil 'rounds' was left at my garden gate.

Action of some sort was required. I telephoned to one parent, passed the word to another by way of the schoolmistress, and the following Saturday all ten members of the Sunday School turned up, each with a trowel. They brought two friends: a small Roman Catholic with a bunch of fair curls, and a long thin agnostic, forbidden by her parents ever to enter a church. Both girls wore shorts and looked far more businesslike than my young Episcopalians. My son carried the sack to the door of the church porch, then retreated for good. I opened it enticingly, drew out a handful of bulbs and tried to remember the Colonel's instructions.

'Try a nice clump over there in the corner at the foot of the tower.' I handed several bulbs to the oldest and brightest member, who was back before I could secure the attention of the boys: 'The ground's

too hard and I can't get the spade in.' I sent her farther away with
the agnostic who, I was sure, had come only to gossip and distract.
Then I started off three obedient brothers against the wall beyond
the tombstones where a shaft of sunlight falls. My daughter Louise
and the rector's son were soon digging round the roots of an ancient
yew, hoping Scottish daffodils would be used to growing without sun.
William was playing catch with the largest bulb he could find; he
grinned cheerfully at me. His younger sister fiddled round me with
the little Catholic. I gave each a few bulbs and pointed to a distant
tree.

A mellow autumn sun cast a pleasant light, and I got out my
camera to focus on the young moles, trying to get as many as possible
into one picture. But before I could take a photograph young Mary
was with me; she had planted a bulb at the far end. Would I come
and look? I walked all the way across, admired her work and
returned to watch the three brothers travelling fast to and fro
between sack and wall. The youngest explained: 'Trying to see how
many we can get into each hole.' His brother nodded: 'I got fifty in
one.'

Mary arrived to say she had planted a second bulb for me to see.
My daughter straightened her back to ask why I wasn't planting any;
the rector's son continued his digging without looking up. Mary's
small sister came with her on the next visit, asking which way up

they went. William continued to play catch. Members of the village passed by and gave advice. Interest was flagging, so I suggested a letter to the donor to be written by Louise and signed by everyone; I could bear her reproachful glances no longer and took her trowel. Writing took a long time; Mary refused to let her Catholic friend sign: 'You don't come here, do you? So you can't write too, can you?' Only the three brothers were at work, and the sack was still half full. 'Do you feel like finishing the sack now?' They didn't.

An elderly gardener passed and shook his head: 'Daffy leaves will look all over the place come June. Proper untidy, they'll be then.'

'Never mind the competition', I smiled bravely; 'they'll look fine in March, won't they, children?' But they had all wandered off except my daughter and the rector's son. 'You've gone and done it again, Mum.'

She was right; the next year we sank to third place. Not that the village worried; they still believed we were second because the notice on the board gave the previous season's judging. But the gallant Colonel had a final word with me: 'Well, at least you've made a start. I'll get some crocuses for you this autumn, and snowdrops. And you can begin on the flowering shrubs in the spring.'

Drawings by R. Grimshaw

The Philosophy of Picking Blackberries   by Joyce Cathcart

There is nothing like blackberrying for restoring the mind. Until a year or two ago people went blackberrying simply for fun, and because it is nice to be gainfully employed out of doors on a fine day, and because blackberries are delicious to eat and cost nothing. But nowadays more and more people are coming to realise that blackberrying is unrivalled as an occupational therapy for the relief of mental stress. If you have reached the stage of knowing that round the next bend, or half-way up the next wall, madness awaits you, then spend half an hour among the blackberry bushes, and you will begin to wonder what all the fuss was about.

It is something to do with the actual physical act of picking and gathering that calms you down; and wooding, that other old country pursuit, is good too, but unfortunately it can lead to destructive addiction. Eager elderly ladies sometimes become rather carried away, and will tear up insecure private fences as booty, and this is anti-social. It is also illegal, so blackberrying is best; and then blackberry bushes are the right height and make less demands upon the internal structural complexities of the middle-aged than the gathering up of wood from the ground.

This posture factor also automatically rules out bilberry picking, because, delicious though the berries are, the prolonged crouching among the low bushes results in ultimate immobility, and so they should be left for the very young, and birds.

Huddling among the homely comforts of placid hedges helps; feeling the undemanding calm of copse and wood, the stabilising effect of huge sheltering trees that are tolerant and enduring and urbane. But industry is the real core of the cure, and it does not matter whether you are content to potter quietly, picking strictly within your reach, or whether you are an avid grabber after the juiciest giants on far-flung tentacles. Still, you must be careful that acquisitiveness does not become dominant, or you will find yourselves back where you started, with an added and ragingly compulsive picking obsession.

Once you have accepted blackberrying as your occupational therapy you will find that it falls into three main categories, Early Morning, Afternoon, and Evening, and it is only by trial and error that you will decide which one keeps you sanest longest.

Early morning blackberrying is suitable for those whose mental trauma responds best to shock treatment, for it contains many stimulating hazards, and for this you will need physical stamina, adequately water-repellent clothing, and a good thick stick. You will find that in early morning at blackberry-picking time everything in sight has been festooned with small silver cobwebs, as though all the old ladies in the world had thrown their hair-nets away over night, and this will beguile you. You will also discover that everything is

The morning picker

wringing wet, as drenching cascades are unleashed over you each time you touch so much as a leaf; and that some domestic animals are particularly inquisitive and aggressive before breakfast, and they will constitute the main hazards.

Horses, looming up at you through swirling morning mists, affect fey attitudes, and have a quirky sense of humour. It can be disconcerting if you have safely negotiated a wet and treacherous nettle-stuffed ditch, and are poised on the opposite bank among a mass of superlative blackberries, to find yourself gazing through a frail barrier of willow-wands into the larky faces of a couple of horses with the wind in their ears.

If you say to them 'Go away', and they go not, and you know that quite soon you are going to overbalance, and fall through the frail willows and land among their massed legs and hooves, you must resist the urge to shout at them rudely and angrily, but withdraw and proceed backwards through the treacherous ditch.

Cows may be encountered, but are rarely argumentative, and are slow-moving if not static. Their sense of humour is undeveloped, but they do care for practical jokes, the most rewarding for them being the well-concealed cow-pat which sends you skating across the dew-soaked grass in a wild and ungainly *pas seul*. There will be a brief pause in the rhythmic rotation of their jaws while they enjoy this sight. Should you, however, dislocate your shoulder, and upset a filled basket, and ruin your clothes with ineradicable dark brown stains, then they will slowly raise and lower their eyelids in silent ecstasy, and collapse slowly, knees first, on the grass.

Young heifers and bullocks are less static, but need not worry early morning pickers much, as incipient rodeos are easily checked by generous brandishing gestures with your good thick stick.

With all these animals about it is a moot point whether you should take your dog along with you on early morning expeditions; unfamiliar and didactic dogs can irritate both cows and horses if they are not kept strictly under control, and if they are, they cause a certain amount of restriction on your picking activities.

There is little hazard to be expected from wild animals since they prudently keep themselves to themselves. But a view of a fox on his stealthy homeward way, or better still, the sight and sound of a vixen

Afternoon picker

seeing off a too-long dependent cub, while splitting her lungs with
her whole blood-curdling repertoire, is something to set you up for
the entire winter. Badgers, who are great blackberry pickers and
eaters themselves and consequently level-headed animals, are seldom
out and about after sunrise.

In the morning there is always the possibility of mushrooms, and
mushrooming may well be the ultimate cure-all. Magical, fairy,
unpredictable delights, conceived by moonlight, and earth-begotten,
they push their indomitable way through the cool grass, like small
cold thumbs in white kid gloves. To walk home to breakfast with a
basketful of glistening blackberries, topped with a pale mound of
mushrooms, is balm to any mind.

People who prefer to pick their blackberries in the afternoon are
never more than superficially unbalanced; their worries surface
easily, and their troubles are temporary. They like to feel the sun
warm on their back, and may soon become inert. They prefer the
smell, rather than the actual picking, of sun-warmed blackberries,
which is to them like a foretaste, or foresmell, of the pie they hope to
bake, or the jelly they hope to boil.

They are, however, keen pickers of pretty well anything that may possibly come in for home decoration. For this all is grist to their mill, from great shaggy, colourless seedheads of hemlock and hogweed and fools' parsley, to small indeterminate and often repellent bits of rotten bark, which may be useful. Should they by chance come upon the bewitching sight of a spindle tree, its lanterns aglow with colour from palest flamingo pink to deepest coral, they must try to remember, before their emotions overcome them, that they are supposed to be undergoing a remedial course of mental therapy.

Whereas early morning pickers will add garment to garment, afternoon pickers tend to remove their clothing. Many an old knitted cardigan has been lost forever, hung like a harp on some forgotten willow tree, and valuable nylons, removed in order to be preserved, have been left behind to decompose in remote and quiet ditches.

It has been known for some public-spirited bird-watcher to be startled by a pair of sad and greying stays, abandoned behind an unobtrusive bush where he has been about to erect his camera-tripod. Murder? he quietly murmurs to himself, or something worse? and he will conscientiously carry his macabre trophy to the nearest police station, for details to be entered formally in a book to do with missing persons. But more than likely it was only some blackberrying Mum, perspiring and muddled.

Intellectual, artistic and creative people, whose minds fairly easily become disordered, may well be, unfortunately for themselves, antagonistic towards all occupational therapies; and this is a pity, because they would benefit more than most from a quiet spell among the bramble bushes. But sometimes they can be inveigled into taking up a basket and a hooked stick, and setting off for an evening blackberrying reconnaissance, seeing in it a good excuse for a loitering, solitary brooding period, away from their anxious loved ones; and the basket and stick are useful as evidence of their good intent and of their respectability.

They will stride briskly away among the lengthening shadows, up the hillside to where the larch plantation stands dark against the changing evening sky, and blue mists weave among the branches. But once out of sight of loving eyes their pace slackens, and they look about for the nearest gate upon which to lean. Should they by chance

Evening picker

see and recognise a blackberry bush, they may go through a few
sketchy blackberry picking motions, but their minds will soon
wander, and they will turn back to the gate for a prolonged and
un-interrupted think.

These intellectually over-wrought types are instantly recognisable,
and should they be chanced upon in the twilight, no attempt should
be made to pass the time of day: for behind the immobile face, the
vacant stare, God only knows what chaos seethes, what train of
thought may be destroyed. For writers can become entangled in an
unmanageable maze of words, and painters can mislay their inward
eye, and musicians can be submerged in a morass of in-
comprehensible harmonies, and no human hand can help them.

Inspiration is a capricious gift, arbitrarily withheld, and
unaccountably bestowed, but even so, while leaning on his gate in the
vicinity of tranquil blackberry bushes, the problems of the
pseudo-blackberrier may be resolved sooner than he hoped; unknown
forces and influences may be at work.

Presently there may be a disturbance among the larches, as a
vague pale shape glides silently away, and a white owl's feather floats

quietly down and down; and as he watches it fall, suddenly, out of the blue, the answer comes, the jig-saw fits, and everything falls into place. The nearest and dearest to whom he will return, after dark but in time for supper, will observe the empty basket, but will know from the feather talisman, so jauntily stuck in his hat, that all is well again, and a sigh of relief will be breathed.

For blackberries are by no means the main objects of these therapeutic exercises, and mushrooms, spindle trees, and white owls' feathers are the bonuses, the gilt on the gingerbread, the cadenzas that enrich the movement.

Drawings by Anne Micke

Sorcerer's Apprentice   by Moya Dewar

My father made medicines, ointments and pills from the herbs gathered as he roamed the countryside on his ancient bicycle. As soon as I was of an age to distinguish a dandelion from a buttercup he commenced my initiation. I was very conscious of my importance as part of the mystery; it put me one up on my friends.

We lived in a small old-fashioned town with a bi-weekly market where itinerant vendors of herbs and medicines would sometimes set up a stall. They were wonderful entertainers and first-rate psychologists. In the trade they were known as 'crocuses'. They would launch into their pattern, frighten the lives out of their audiences with horrifying details of the diseases that awaited them and then, as the symptoms began to manifest themselves, move in with their cures at a shilling a bottle. Sales were usually pretty brisk in those pre-National Health days. They had their gimmicks too. One always kept his herb-gathering hand gloved – to maintain its purity, he said. Another drew his crowd by waving a flashing sword round his head and then neatly splitting a potato held on the outstretched hand of some local volunteer.

Part of my job as sorcerer's apprentice was to keep an eye on the crocuses and report to my father any new arrival. I would wriggle my way to the front of the crowd, note what was being sold and the manner of selling, and try to estimate how much money was taken at

Those Leaves Again

by Arnold Wiles

'You didn't complain about picking up my apples'

'I always let the worms pull mine into the ground'

The trivial round

'Good Lord! How long have you been up there?'

each session. It was a fascinating job. By the time I was ten I had a good working knowledge of the human anatomy and a stock of coarse stories that would have astounded a navvy. Most of the crocuses did a one-night stand and were not seen again, but if any looked like making our town a regular port of call, Father would investigate personally. If they were genuine he would leave them alone, unless they happened to have some remedy he had not yet come across, when he would hound them until they parted with their secret. He was very overpowering. I remember an insurance agent once calling to sell us a policy and leaving fifteen minutes later with a dazed look and a bottle of blood tonic. Being a bit of a rogue himself, Father was quick to detect signs of chicanery in others. When he made up his mind to drive a crocus off his stamping ground it was sure to be a battle royal.

There were two fellows I especially remember. One called himself a gypsy and went under a famous Romany name. He ran for about three weeks before Father decided his hour had come. The gypsy was offering a bottle of medicine positively guaranteed to cure gall-stones, kidney trouble, disturbed nights and cirrhosis of the liver. He named all the herbs that had gone into the making of this mixture, with lurid stories of the rites of gathering them. How often I heard about the mandrake that shrieked in agony as its roots were pulled up! Then came a bull-like roar from Father, and he slapped his thigh triumphantly. The gypsy had mentioned among his ingredients two herbs whose actions were diametrically opposed; one was a laxative, the other a specific for tightening up the bowels. I never heard Father in finer form than on that day. By the time he had finished enlarging on the state of the human gut after these two herbs had worked their stop-go action, the audience was in stitches and the gypsy choking with rage. He left and we never saw him again.

The other fellow lasted a little longer – about a month, I think – and this time I was brought in to help. He was clever, he seemed genuine, his patter was faultless and Father had not been able to catch him out. He was doing well too. We saw people returning for more boxes of pills, and yet Father's nose was twitching: the unmistakable smell of trickery was there. When we spotted an old woman who had bought Father's embrocation for years handing over

'The audience was in stitches and the gypsy choking with rage'

her shilling for pills, he knew the time had come for desperate
measures. He bought a box of pills himself and took them home for
investigation. They were pure soap with a coloured sugar coating.

Next market day we waited behind the obelisk till our crocus had
gathered a sizeable crowd and then we moved in, Father with his
shilling to buy more pills, and myself well hidden behind him with a
bottle of water, basin and clay pipe. When the man had finished and
people were just going to step up for their pills, Father gave his usual
bellow, which stopped them in their tracks. Then with a grandiose
bow to the crocus he handed over his shilling, took a box of pills and
tipped them into the bottle of water I handed to him. This he shook
violently before pouring the contents into the white basin which I
was holding out like an acolyte. He hoisted me on to the stall and,
trembling with excitement, I dipped my little clay pipe into the
mixture and blew a gorgeous fat iridescent bubble. It floated lazily
above the crowd and headed for the Town Hall.

There was a dead silence as all heads turned to follow the progress of the soap-bubble. The crocus stood with a look of stupefied cunning on his face, his hands full of pillboxes. Father broke the silence with another roar, 'Yah, soapy pills! Soapy pills!' I blew bubbles like a thing possessed. Some burst in my face, children jumped round trying to catch them, the mixture slopped down the front of my dress, there was laughter and catcalling, and above all Father's voice bellowing 'So-o-apy pills!' The pandemonium brought the market inspector at a scurry, and a three-cornered argument ensued. I continued blowing bubbles: the wonder was that there could be so many. Doubtless the few soap-flakes Father had put in the bottle helped.

The fun came to an end at last and we marched off in triumph, half the crowd following us. My clay pipe was dropped and trodden on, but what a fortune in pennies I collected! Looking back I caught the eye of the discomfited quack. He shrugged his shoulders, opened his case and started packing.

Drawing by Brian Walker

Kill or Cure   by F. J. Archer

The doctor lived in a three-storey Victorian house in our West Midland village. Experienced and in an old-fashioned way well qualified, he was not only the village physician but also district council chairman, guardian of the poor and J.P.; and he presided over the school board and the parish council. As late as the early 1920s he drove round the village in a high trap, his son acting as horseman. To his patients he always stressed how ill they had been, and how he had cured them; and the older villagers swore by him.

The surgery window adjoined the village street, and the doctor could be seen with his Edward VII beard and a smoking-cap, dispensing his medicines. As official doctor of a local benefit society, he used to vet applicants there. When three young men of my acquaintance called on him one winter's evening, he told them to strip off and went round them with a lighted candle, dripping hot wax over them *en route*. The blinds were not drawn, to the delight of a group of village youths in the road.

Walter, our ploughman, visited the surgery with a poisoned finger which needed lancing. 'Put your hand over that table', he was told; and the doctor tried to cut the blister with a pair of rusty scissors. Eventually he succeeded, spoiling his polished table in the process, and told the patient to keep plenty of linseed oil on the finger; he seemed to know nothing about hygiene. When my grandmother broke her leg, he did not set it but pulled it about so much that the pain caused her to twist the iron bed-post.

On one occasion a farmer called and was invited in for a drink. When he saw the doctor reach to the top shelf for one of several blue bottles marked 'Poison', he exclaimed: 'I'm not having whisky out of that, doctor.' His host reassured him with the explanation that he could not keep whisky in the house unless it was so labelled.

The doctor enjoyed a bit of shooting and sometimes visited patients with a gun under his arm, as if to kill or cure. One day he was going up the village street with his gun when he was told of a stag gazing on his land at the top of the hill. Arriving there just before dusk, he crept up under a tall hedge next to an orchard and fired both barrels at an object which turned out to be a cow crib. A few days later, when the rag-and-bone man called at the pub, the landlord sent him over to the house, telling him there was a fine deerskin there. The doctor was furious.

When he travelled to council meetings and petty sessions, he always started late for the train. Dressed in black overcoat and black box-hat, he would pass my house in the trap at the canter, his son standing on the shafts with whip in hand, shouting to the pony at the top of his voice. By this time the train would be almost in the station, and I have known the son to drive alongside the rails by the siding so that his father could board it from there.

Local people usually owed the doctor money and, as elections approached, he would visit his patients saying: 'If you don't vote for me, I shall send my bill in.' He was never unseated.

The Season of the Year   by Arnold Wiles

'Please may we get our ball back?'

'Seen the bootscraper?'

'Look what I've found, dear!'

'Mother just phoned. She's coming for the weekend'

The Motorway Cometh   by H. F. Ellis

The advance of the monster can no longer be ignored. 'Advance', with its suggestion of a steady progression, is perhaps not the right word. 'Spasmodic manifestations' would be a better description of what one sees as the M5 feels its way south-west through north Somerset.

Years ago, travelling by train from New York to Boston, I had the good fortune to meet a new highway or thruway which was heading in the other direction, on a course more or less parallel with the railroad. This really was an advance. In front, like the vanguard of some expedition cutting its way through virgin bamboo forests, marched giant machines uprooting large trees and tossing them aside like matchsticks. Then came the earth-movers, scraping off here, depositing there, as the terrain and the engineers' gradient plans dictated; behind them the drainage crews with pipes; and after that the consolidators, the metalling men, the painters of white lines. All along the route, as my train swept by, the highway was visibly growing from infancy to maturity, visibly moving from Boston to New York. If I were in the mood for exaggeration I would add that

the last glimpse I had of it, before road and rail parted, showed a queue of traffic patiently following up the final batch of workers; but I will content myself with noting that the combined speed of train and highway, where they first met, was enough to cause a perceptible shock-wave.

Here in Somerset the procedure is different, more bitty. The man with a wheelbarrow, toiling away at what will be for the present the terminal point at Edithmead near Burnham-on-Sea, would be disappointed if he could see how little of the bridge over the Avon twenty miles farther back, on which all depends, has (at the time of writing) arisen. There is an absence of that sense of juggernaut inevitability with which an American highway unrolls across the countryside. We prefer, it seems, to begin at each end, like men making a tunnel through the Alps, in the confident hope that the two parties will one day meet in the middle – 'with an error of less than half an inch', as the papers always say. On the M4, the outposts near Maidenhead and Pucklechurch (is it?) have been hoping for some years.

All the same the advance of the M5 can no longer be ignored; and now a curious thing is happening. For a long time there has been, with reason, a great outcry in the South-West about the neglect of our road systems and the hideous accumulation of summer traffic jams. Evil communications, it is rightly said, have corrupted good manners. So you would think that a considerable leap forward, like this approach of the motorway to the heart of Somerset, would be hailed with relief and joy. Not entirely. As the day draws nearer, a note of alarm begins to be heard. One is reminded of a visit, long expected, from some relative from distant parts. For months, years, there has been eager anticipation. What fun it will be to have Aunt Hester with us after all this time! It will take us out of ourselves. So good for the children. All sorts of expeditions, to all sorts of places we have never bothered to see, will be arranged.

But when a feeling of imminence creeps on, when the actual date of arrival is fixed and fast approaching, doubts appear. What will she be like? We know so little about her. Will she bring poodles? How, in short, are we going to support so fearful an upheaval in our accustomed way of life?

That Dream Cottage

by Arnold Wiles

'They won't buy the place either, but at least we're getting rid of a lot of our old apples'

'Good solid walls, none of your jerry building'

'What's it to be, rising damp now or rising prices later?'

'Tell you what. I'll throw in a dozen bottles of home-made parsnip wine.'

'A grave threat exists to Mendip and the Somerset coastline from
the people who will swarm to the West Country on the M4 and the
M5.' So, not long ago, spoke a nature conservationist; and he added,
my local paper tells me, these formidable words: 'Twenty-five million
people will be within three hours' drive of north Somerset and, as
long as the motorways stops at Edithmead, people will disperse from
there into the surrounding countryside.' Twenty-five million people
on a day trip, with paper bags and all!

Of course, when the motorway, like a wounded snake, has dragged
its slow length along to its ultimate destination, relief will be at hand.
Somerset will breathe again. For then, surely, the twenty-five million
will sweep on into defenceless Cornwall; and we shall live – some of
us – to bless the great highway for draining off from our towns the
endless stream of vehicles that, from May to September, turn places
like Bridgwater and Taunton into clangorous infernos. A quiet
parochial peace will descend upon us again while, out of sight and
out of mind, those interminable Birmingham number-plates go by.

Not so again, apparently. There will be, a Taunton highway
authority has lately declared, 'some temporary relief'; but soon the
increasing ease of communications with places far afield will so swell
the numbers of those who come to visit, to trade, to settle in our
midst, that our streets will again be chock-a-block from morn to
night. The whole town will no doubt have to be razed to the ground
to provide parking space for this irresistible multitude. Perhaps we
ought never to have invited Auntie in the first place.

One must try, however, to keep calm. Can it in fact be true that at
stage one, when the M5 ends at Edithmead, twenty-five million
motorists will exude from the terminus over neighbouring Sedgemoor
and the Quantocks, like a blob of ink or like the bubble of mercury at
the bottom of a thermometer tube; as if the dread signboard 'End of
Motorway' were an angel with a flaming sword barring further
progress to the South-West? After all, the M4 at present ends at
Newport, and I have heard no cry from those parts that the valley of
the Usk will soon be overwhelmed by countless hordes of picnickers.

The analogy has its flaws, I am aware. More consoling may be the
reflection that the West (and any other part of the country for that
matter) has in its time faced and survived an invasion threat that

must have been more terrible in prospect than anything the motorway can offer. I mean the rail. Here was no gradually increasing influx of repulsive visitors such as the motoring age has brought, no question of a mere couple of hours' reduction in travelling time between London or the Midlands and the West. With terrifying speed the railways raced across the countryside, bifurcating, sending out tentacles as they went, seeking out even the smallest centres of population, so that hardly a hamlet could consider itself safe. Almost overnight, or anyway within a few years after the start of the 1840s, the seething masses of the Metropolis (not hitherto great mail-coach users) found themselves less than half a day's journey from such unheard-of places as Bath and Exeter.

The Great Western reached Bristol from Paddington in 1841. By 1844 it was at Exeter, *via* Taunton. Was there not then, at some intermediate date when the line was approaching the halfway mark between Bristol and Exeter, a panic fear among Tauntonians that millions of gin-sodden Londoners, unable to proceed farther, would ooze out like a miasma over their quiet streets and country lanes? I don't know, but I doubt it.

Opposition to the railways there certainly was: from land-owners, from Wordsworth, from farmers fearful as ever about the effect on their milch cows, but not, apparently, from the populace at large. 'The day of a new railway's opening' (I quote from that entertaining railway writer Canon Roger Lloyd) 'was always a tremendously popular occasion, with cheering crowds lining every inch of the way, and an opulent feast in a tent with free drinks for the privileged at the end of it.' They were in favour of progress in those days.

The people of Somerset will not, I fear, line every inch of the M5 from the Avon to Edithmead when the opening day dawns. They will not, on the other hand, be utterly cast down. More cars will be a nuisance, once they get off the motorway. But more cars mean more visitors, and more visitors mean more money. And if their numbers threaten to become insupportable, we might borrow an idea from the Isle of Wight and charge a small fee at the border. Would £2 to come in be reasonable? It would be awkward, of course, if Devon made it £10 to go out.

Drawing by Brian Walker

Ode to Millicent or Franciscus Redivivus   by Martin Thornton

Illustrated by Arnold Wiles

I was digging up potatoes in the garden of the Rectory,
In cold October sunshine, working steadily along,
Neither burdened by the labour nor the time that it would take me,
All enveloped in potatoes; millipedes; another row.
I was digging up potatoes in the garden of the Rectory;
Forget-me-not, convolvulus, more millipedes, and dock;
I was digging up potatoes, when I stopped.

And lit my pipe.

So I meandered, daydreamed, convolvulus and smoke rings,
Bird songs, thistledown, millipedes and daisies,
Men and ladies, boys and girls, convolvulus and babies,
I was digging up potatoes: when I stopped.

For God said stop.

And millipede stopped.

And God said: Benedicte! I wish to introduce Miss Millicent Pede.

And I said: Good afternoon Miss Pede.

And she said: Shall I sing you a song?

And I said: Yes please.

So she sang:

> This is a song that has never been sung
> Since the dawn of creation, when things first began.
> God conceived me, designed me, and gave me legs: one –
> And ninety-nine others in case that went wrong;
> The Trinity made me, with infinite care,
> With other such creatures his friendship to share;
> For He's fond of me, loving me all of my life,
> And He also made rabbits and maggots and mice,
> And bears and black-beetles and lizards and lice.
> It's marvellous, too, that He also produces
> Donkeys and ducks and remarkable gooses,
> And Einstein and Schweitzer and Liebniz and Paine
> And Martha and Mary and Emily Jane.
> Yet the infinite glory I'm sure you'll concede
> Is that God is so fond of Miss Millicent Pede.

Then I dug some more potatoes in the garden of the Rectory,
In cold October sunshine, working steadily along.
I felt elevated, edified, incomparably comforted,
Excited, thrilled, and sanctified by Sister Milly's song.

I have dug up lots of learning in the lecture room and library,
In dull December darkness reading rapidly along,
I have read about the attributes ascribed to the Divinity
By Paul and Mark and Matthew, Thomas and Tertullian,
I must hasten to refresh my mind, by Bellarmine or Bede:
But the God whom I can worship is the One who loves Miss Pede.

'It's Rawhide'

by Hywel

Autumn Tail Corn

WEST-COUNTRY landlady to prospective tenant who had admired her fine honeysuckle bush: 'Ah, but you should see it in the summer-time, Mrs Brown; the stench fairly ruptures you'.

ULSTER countrywoman, describing encounter with fierce dog: 'It kept goin' in devourin' circles around me'.

EYING the clay soil fast dried under wind and hot sun, a Hertfordshire gardener commented: 'That looks that white and spiteful'.

NEAR a baby welfare centre a mother was accounting for her infant's tears: 'I've just taken him to be humanised'.

HOUSE physician in provincial hospital, to old lady who has had a rigor: 'Did your teeth chatter?' Old lady: 'I didn't take that notice, doctor; they were on the locker'.

SOMERSET farmer irritated by too cheerful wife, 'Many a bird that sings before seven cat du 'av 'im by eleven'.

SOMERSET house-painter, sheltering from storm, of householder rejoicing at the good the rain would do her garden: 'That woman would drown anyone for a cabbage'.

HEREFORDSHIRE farmer giving small boy a bag of apples, 'Ere ye be, give 'em to yer mam. Tell 'er they be too sour to yet, and they wunna cook, but they be real good keepers'.

OLD GLASGOW woman, watching a new battery being put in the radio, 'Is that whit gies it the piff tae gang?'

CORNISH farm worker, looking up at stormy sky: ''E be 'eavin' down they 'ails brave an' 'ard'.

AS he unloaded manure, a Co. Dublin farm worker commented on his tractor: 'Her hand brake used to be quite good, but it won't pull the stockin's on a dead man now'.

CORNISH farmer, blaming modern education for his inability to get an assistant milker: 'If we breed all race-'orses, where do we get the 'orse to put in the mangel-cart?'

HAMPSHIRE woman, to visiting parson who has congratulated her sick husband on getting downstairs to the parlour: ''E ain't no better, sir, but we fetched 'im down, 'cause we thought 'twould be so orkerd bringin' the coffin down them there stairs'.

LEICESTERSHIRE woman, of someone who worked slowly, 'He's too slow to carry cold dinners'.

AN old carter, seeing rooks soaring on upward air currents, remarked, 'Look at they old rooks busy making willow baskets'.

A COUNTRYMAN in Kincardineshire recognised a friend and said,

'Aye, aye! and fit like?' 'Aw weel, just sic like!' replied his friend.

CORNISH farmer in village shop, surprised to find bill less than he expected: 'Well, 'tidn' no scattin' job, sure nuff!' ['Scat': to break in pieces, hence to bankrupt.]

COTSWOLD waller, on receiving load of unsuitable stone: 'They be as big as bullocks' 'eads and as 'ard as Pharaoh's 'eart'.

IRISH labourer on windy day: 'If ye'd lost a shurrt button sure ye'd know 'twas gone'.

ELDERLY Somerset man, passing clump of ivy in flower: 'Hark to they bees an' flies a-charming on the ivy!'

OLD Warwickshire man, attributing hooliganism of village youngsters to attendance at town school: 'Trouble is, they'm double-growed nowadays'.

PERTHSHIRE farm worker to tourist who had been complaining about the wet weather, 'Ye must gang wi things as things gang wi' ye'.

OVERHEARD in a Highland inn: 'Ach; there's folks dyin' now as never died afore'.

YORKSHIRE octogenarian, referring to the poor income of his young days, 'When ivver a bit cum my way it were just like picking (pitching) on t' haystack – there were allus somebody waitin' to take it'.

NORTH Devon countryman, describing to another a chance encounter: "Er looker Oi a look an' Oi looker 'er a look, then Oi says, "Ee it's Nancy" '.

NEW York expression for a bustling woman, 'She's the whole team and the dog under the wagon'.

Winter

Village Hall Play, by George Adamson

Heigh Ho the Holly   by Jack Jennings

As the year grows old and the shortest day approaches, our woodmen
in the Forest of Dean leave timber felling for a few days and turn to
cutting the berried holly which thrives in the damp shade of oaks
planted after the Napoleonic wars. Twigs for cutting should be no
thicker than one's little finger. Buyers from the towns swing the
14-lb. bundles deftly by the strings over the sides of their lorries and
leap up to trample the holly down, complaining the while of its poor
quality.

'This ain't the stuff we want – too prickly, like an 'edge 'og's back.
It's the smooth kind we always buy. We'll 'ave a job to get rid o' this
lot. You want the kids to laugh at Christmas, an' this 'll make 'em
cry. Look at them branches too. Stone the crows! We come 'ere to
buy 'olly, not firewood at forty quid a ton' – and so on. But we ignore
the banter, having heard it all before: it is the dealers' method of
'softening up' before they bargain over the price, and we give as good

as we get. We know there is nothing wrong with our holly; as soon as they have paid for one load, most of them will be asking for another.

These fellows always seem to be working against time; they often arrive late and are in a hurry to be off again. They have a long way to go and, hoping to be first in the market, fear a hold-up in snow, frost or fog. Of course, selling holly and Christmas trees is only a sideline for them; they deal in all sorts of commodities.

Today Charlie and George, bachelor brothers who live with their old father on a small farm in Buckinghamshire, keep us amused as they load up: "'Ad a bit of a shock when we got back last time – October wasn't it? Couldn't find the old man nowhere. 'Unted all over – not a sign of 'im – finished up in the orchard, an' when we 'ollered out the old man answered. Where d' you think 'e was? Up a tree. Bin up a ladder to pick apples an' stepped off on to a fork, an' along come the old sow an' 'er litter an' knocked the ladder down. There was Dad, seventy-two last birthday, left standin' in the fork twelve feet up over an hour. 'E was that cold and stiff. By Gor, wasn't 'e glad to get down!'

We asked the brothers how they manage about food and who cooks for them. 'Oh, we does pretty well', says George. 'We 'ad a 'ousekeeper once, but she was a poor cook. We come back from shootin' one day with a couple o' rabbits, a pheasant, two pigeons and a sparrow-'awk; put 'em on the dairy floor. Well, she cooked the

'Left standin' twelve feet up'

'It began to snort'

rabbits next day an' the pigeons day after that O.K. Wednesday I
went to get the pheasant, 'cause I'd promised it to the chap as 'ad the
shootin'. "What 'appened to that sparrow-'awk?" I asks 'er. "'Awk,"
she says, "what are you talkin' about?" "That bird that was in my
bag with the pigeons," I says, "bird with thin yeller legs an' a sharp
beak an' claws". "Oh, that," she says, "you ate 'im yestiddy".'
 Charlie was a timber cutter once and liked the job, but left it to
join the army. 'I got into trouble with 'is Lordship', he tells us. 'We'd
cut a biggish larch on the estate – about a 'undred an' forty cube.
Twisted as it came down an' landed across a ride. Well, we thought
we'd 'ave a cup o' tea before we trimmed it out, but we'd 'ardly sat
down when 'oo should come along but My Lord on 'orseback. "Shift
that tree!" 'e shouted as soon as 'e clapped eyes on me. "What d' you
think I am," I says, "an elephant?" "Less of your tongue, my lad," 'e
says, "Or I'll put this crop across your backside". "Ah," I says, "then
I'll put this axe through yer neck". Well, years after, 'e was colonel o'
my regiment an' I was up on a charge. "I seem to remember your
face", 'e said. "Where 'ave I seen you before?" I never let on.'
Sometimes the brothers call at remote farms in search of holly. A
few weeks earlier, having left the lorry at a road junction, George
was crossing a field to one such farm when he noticed an irate bull
pacing dangerously near him on the other side of a low stone wall. It
began to snort, so George took a fair-sized stone from the wall and
heaved it at the bull's head. 'Stone 'it 'im bang on 'is 'orn,' says

George, 'an' 'e went straight down like as if 'e'd bin shot. Next week, when I called at the farm, the cows were in the yard an' there in the middle was the old bull with 'is 'orn wrapped in sackin' an' binder twine. "What's the matter with 'im boss?" I asked. "Bin fightin'?" "No," said the farmer, "'e's knocked 'isself somewhere – no good for showin' now. Spoilt 'is 'ead". Better 'is 'ead than mine, I thought to meself.'

By now the load is complete, four tons in all; and we drive down to the sawmill to check the weight and settle up. A bottle is handed round and everyone takes a noisy gulp. 'Was at a place last week,' says Charlie, 'an' the estate foreman 'elped me load. I'd just 'anded 'im 'is Christmas box – 'alf a bottle o' whisky – when the agent comes on the scene. "I d-d-don't w-w-want this", says the foreman. "W-w-what am I g-g-going to do with it?" "Rub it on yer chest", I says an' drives away.' And with that, their load sheeted down, the brothers scrape the mud from the wheels, clean the windscreen and climb into the cab. The diesel engine springs noisily to life, and they are off.

Drawings by Brian Walker

Lo, the Angels   by Rachel Williams

Other people have Christmas. Village school-teachers have nativity plays. From early November and through to the late, dark days of December the village school-teacher feels that this year's nativity play is possibly the most unholy thing to be conceived and produced; that parents, normally indulgent of the efforts of their offspring, will not be able to ignore this year's fiasco; that they will see it as an open invitation to turn to another religion in disgust; that this is the very last nativity play she will attempt; that she is in the wrong profession altogether and next July she will leave and be a shorthand typist.

However, the term progresses inexorably. As December begins the clothes horses are brought out from the headmistress's adjoining house and the by now traditional scenery is touched up and pinned on to them. No one thinks of asking the headmistress how she airs her clothes during December. Village headmistresses bear their discomforts at this time with seemly stoicism. An incredibly sardonic donkey peers over the scenery at a tomato box on legs complete with fifteen-year-old straw, but as yet no inhabitant. The dressing-up box is opened, the giggling angels are fitted up with grubby robes and then take them home under their arms for mother to add a little biological whiteness to the biblical scene. The shepherds tighten their dressing gown cords, and wince as the hand towels are bound round their heads with a vicious pull.

The three wise men empty their mothers' tea caddies for gold and frankincense and the Vicar is approached once more for his ebony box for the myrrh. Their crowns are made from old jewellery and copious gold paint. A huge spangled star is made which, Lo! they will behold in the East. Well, at least one will point and say 'Lo!' The others will be grinning vacantly at the front seats. The angel Gabriel is bigger than the other angels and therefore of a different breed, she feels. She has to be dressed in the redoubtable school cleaner's nightie which is of cream nuns veiling 'and made when people knew how to run and fell' as she observed tartly. Fresh tinsel is bought from the Christmas-orientated shops in the outside world; last year's is tarnished and would be bad for the angelic image.

Rehearsals move slowly. Joseph is often away at the speech clinic and has a script cunningly composed of words without the letter 's'. The angel Gabriel herself is away with what is reported as a 'bladder complaint' despite her superiority. The little shepherds cannot manage their crooks, everyone catches cold; even the girl who is playing Mary sniffs and claps a hanky to her nose as she is asked to lean solicitously over the tomato box.

Dawn breaks on the last Thursday before the Christmas holidays. Night must fall, the teacher tells herself comfortingly, and the shorthand is coming on well.

After lunch the boys put out the chairs in rows for their mothers, aunties, grannies and for the whole tribe of Israel to sit on. The baby doll is laid in the straw for the first time. Everyone is ordered to the outside lavatories, for the last time, as they are warned severely. The job of dressing, pinning and pulling together begins. The whole cast is lined up at the door ready to file into what is inevitably termed a tableau. The teacher surveys the squirming line and cannot

Cold Comfort   **Arnold Wiles surveys the weather**

'What do you think? Shall we put on another twenty-five pence worth – or
go to bed?'

'But you're always complaining that you never get a chance to wear it'

'Of course they couldn't do that before I'd installed the double glazing!'

remember having ever seen such a motley bunch of shepherds, such a shifty-eyed sniffing pair of innkeepers, such a miserable Madonna, surely the most retarded of Wise Men . . . this moment is the nadir of the school-teacher's year.

But now the headmistress starts to play a well-loved carol at the piano for the audience to sing together quietly. This announces the start of proceedings and muffles the sounds of the said tableau forming. As the music begins the angel Gabriel is allowed up to the lavatories by special dispensation owing to the nature of her 'complaint'. A glimpse of grey knee socks is seen as she hauls the nuns veiling round her knees. The teacher, by now anaesthetised to anachronisms and the like, merely breathes a sigh of relief as a flash of tinsel past a back window denotes mission accomplished and a speedy return.

As the music dies away, the screens are removed by two stalwart boys who have been standing behind them waiting for the countdown. The clear voice of one of the bigger girls hangs on the air of the unusually quiet school room. 'And Joseph also went up from Galilee out of the city of Nazareth . . .' The words of the Authorised Bible, so maligned and meaningless over the past few weeks, ring out again this time clearly and truly, subtly enhanced by the soft local accent. A metamorphosis begins and takes shape under its own slow impetus. The school-teacher feels a relaxation in her heart and she knows, as she knows at a certain moment every year, that this will be the fitting climax to the whole country year. These children are probably the best she has had, she thinks proudly, and it is a privilege to be able to work with them for a short part of their lives.

'And Lo the angel of the Lord came upon them . . .' Enter the grey socks bearing the star, which, Lo, they are all looking at. The age-old words of the last carol are sung by everyone, all eyes fixed on the hitherto scorned tableau. The moment is crystallised into a private significance for each person watching. The screens are drawn together for the last time and the miracle which happens every year has taken place once more. Yes, privilege is not too strong a word, thinks the teacher proudly. Moments like these are possibly not experienced by shorthand typists.

Painful Extraction   by E. Lovekin

I was about twelve years old and staying alone with Granny when I had a most appalling toothache. She said, 'I know a very good chemist who takes teeth out', and we promptly set off for the shop. An old man, wearing a beautiful skull-cap of black velvet embroidered with coloured flowers, invited us into a room at the back, sat me down, had a look at my tooth and put a pair of ear-phones on my head. As he talked earnestly to Granny, I could hear nothing but an Edison Bell recording of a rather noisy band from the wax cylinder on an old-fashioned phonograph.

When the ear-phones were removed Granny said, 'You shall have a shilling if you don't cry'. That should have warned me. The chemist dabbed my tooth and gums with ether and proceeded to fit the dental key (I still have it). It was quite a common instrument in those days: a type of hinged corkscrew, the ebony handle set at right-angles to the steel shaft and a hook also at right-angles to it. The old man placed the hook over the molar and, with the shaft lying along the side of the jaw, rotated the handle away from it, so that something had to give. I did not cry. I was too shocked. The pain penetrated the depth of my soul, and the world rocked around me to the sound of crushing bone. When the old man produced a two-fanged molar with a piece of bone attached, his pride was great.

Near the chemist's shop was a greengrocer's with baskets of fruit and vegetables displayed outside. One skip full of egg-plums caught my eye as we passed, and I took a flying kick at it. After that I felt much better. I looked back to see plums scattered all over the pavement and roadway; and Granny, the irate shopkeeper and several passers-by picking them up.

'You are a very naughty boy', said Granny when she caught up with me. 'I have had to buy seven pounds of damaged plums.' I nursed my jaw, wiped blood from my mouth and said nothing. As we neared home she said in a more conciliatory tone, 'Did it hurt much, dear?' Again I remained silent, letting her surmise the worst.

The next day she produced from the oven a huge earthenware casserole, with glazed top and handles, took off the cover and, lifting it down to my level, said, 'Smell!' At that moment the bottom dropped out of the casserole, and we both got our feet scalded. Cold stewed plums and custard appeared on the table for days afterwards. Granny never wasted anything.

Rural Feet   by Margaret Macbrair

The benefits of the welfare state are slowly being absorbed by country dwellers. Relief for elderly feet has reached our village: a voluntary organisation in the nearest city has a grant to administer, so we are to have a chiropodist twice a month for those of pensionable age. The village hall has been booked; volunteers are out with tea and biscuits; but trouble lies ahead. Our efficient urban benefactor thinks in lunar terms, four weeks to a month; the village lives by the calendar month. First and third Tuesdays or Thursdays or Sundays make admirable points for fixing Women's Institute meetings, the collection of rubbish bins or early celebrations of Holy Communion. So chiropody, as it takes place in the village hall, must follow the local rhythm and do likewise. But how can we combine with a neighbouring village which has already inexplicably agreed to bow its head to urban authority and have its sessions every second week?

Saxon and Norman may be blamed for our erratic boundaries, eccentric seventeenth-century squires for winding roads and the confused jumble of cottages, but the origin of this latest dilemma goes much farther back, to our ancestors' acceptance of the Roman calendar. Up to now the countryman, older and wiser than the citizen, has quietly secreted those extra two or three days at the end of each month. Even at those great questioning times, nightly in the village pub or annually at the parish meeting, no-one asked what the drivers of the rural district council's rubbish vans did on fifth Thursdays. Now people may wonder what our chiropodist does with her extra days, and then start probing the lives of others. But we shall stick to our first and third Tuesdays, though I can foresee much telephoning and arranging, much fumbling with diaries in town and country, endless notes and messages to puzzled pensioners in remote cottages — all because one village has weakly agreed to toe the lunar line.

Local History   **by Veronica Bamfield**

I was not sure of the way, so I pulled up hopefully at the end of the lane. The building which loomed enormous and shadowy in the dark proved to be the village hall. Opening the door to an unaccustomed rush of warmth, I found a little old man rattling away at a stove which glowed red all over.

'Evenin'', he said. 'What are we havin' tonight?'

'I've been asked to talk on local history', I told him.

'Oh, ay. Well, you couldna say there was much of it round here', he went on, dismissing my hectic stop-gap homework with a friendliness I could not resent.

When the class had assembled I explained that the regular tutor was ill and handed round the register, noticing once again and with pleasure how the old names turn up in all walks of life and in every part of the county. Among the thirty present there was an encouraging number of men, for in many villages, evening classes, like church-going, are considered the woman's business.

I always leave at least a third of the time for the class themselves to contribute, so I ended my talk brightly with 'Now, the meeting is yours'. Then I waited, but not for long. A small dark man in his sixties rose at the back: 'My grandad killed a man in Critton Wood'.

There was a creaking and shuffling as twenty-nine bodies turned in their chairs. 'Oh, Mr Stringer!' a little woman in a mouse-coloured hat exclaimed. 'How nice!' I was about to add, but I managed 'How thrilling!'

Mr Stringer leaned back and looked all round the room. 'Grandfather was a gamekeeper, see', he confided, 'keeper to old Sir Alfred. One night 'e was down Critton and caught this chap poachin'. Knew 'im well. Warned 'im several times 'e 'ad, but there 'e was red-'anded, so 'e strangled 'im like'.

No word was spoken as the whole class stared in my direction. 'And was he never caught?' I asked.

'No, an' it wouldn't never 'ave come out, only 'e took fright an' told on 'is dyin' bed'.

'What about the body?' someone inquired.

'Oh, ay, they found the body, but they never pinned it down on anyone, see'.

The silence was now complete, and I had no option but to wind up the meeting.

Early Telephone Days
by Beatrice Reid

Sixty years ago we lived near Brighton and there was no telephone in the village, so my father wrote to the manager of the Bell Telephone Company to say there were several people who wanted one. The reply was that a line from the Brighton exchange would be connected if he would guarantee twelve subscribers. The annual charge would be £3 for unlimited local calls. Installation would be free, and there was no such thing as rental. We soon got our twelve subscribers, including the doctor, the grocer, the butcher and the major, a retired cavalry officer whose chief occupation was backing horses.

There was much speculation as to where the exchange would be, and this was settled a few weeks later when the butcher's boy announced that the pole for the line from Brighton had arrived. He had seen it that morning on a long trailer drawn by a horse. At that moment men were digging a hole in the backyard of one of the houses in Albert Road. Sure enough the little front room of a terraced house occupied by Mr and Mrs Martin and their baby became the exchange. Mrs Martin was to be our operator. It was not long before the pole was used as a heaven-sent attachment for her neighbour's clothes-line, while her own baby's small garments fluttered from the guy cables.

A few more poles appeared in the village as the subscribers were connected, and when our turn came we decided to have the instrument, no ornament on any consideration, in the cloakroom. My father, being a very tall man, had it fixed to the wall to suit his height. This caused a certain amount of annoyance as he was hardly ever at home. A large block of wood was placed on the floor on which the other members of the family stood in order to reach the mouthpiece and turn the handle to call the operator. It had not

Christmas Cards for Country People

by Arnold Wiles

The parson

The policeman

The veterinary surgeon

The housewife

The crofter's wife

The village engineer

occurred to anyone at that date to sit down while telephoning. A personal directory hung on a hook near by, until it fell to the floor and was chewed up by one of the dogs. After that numbers were written on the wall around the telephone. The wall could never be repainted.

The large cloakroom was lit by a gas jet. After dark we never knew which should come first, lighting the gas or answering the telephone. Often there were important messages for my father which he insisted should be written down accurately. The room contained the usual paraphernalia; a long wooden box for the croquet set, greatcoats, raincoats, satchels and so forth on the pegs, and a thick, furlined, camel-hair coat used by my father when driving the dog-cart in winter. It was past its prime, but was reprieved from the jumble sale by my mother who in the cold weather always wore it when telephoning. She told everybody to do this; it was known as the telephone coat.

We all got on well with Mrs Martin. Our first call of the day was frequently preceded by 'How's the baby?' When his first tooth appeared we were duly informed. She knew who our friends were, and would sometimes tell us their whereabouts. Once when I was arranging a tennis four she told me that Miss Wilson had gone to Brighton on the ten and would be back on the twelve. The clatter of crockery was sometimes heard, as though she were making her pastry alongside the switchboard. On one occasion when my sister and I had gone to a party in Brighton, we telephoned home at about midnight to say that we had missed the last train (though actually we had never intended catching it). When we got home next morning my mother told us to pick a basket of strawberries and take it to Mrs Martin with an apology for ringing so late.

Albert, her husband, took over the switchboard on Sundays and some evenings. Albert had a bored, irritated voice, as though we had interrupted him from reading the evening paper. Occasionally we would hear an unfamiliar voice explaining that Mrs Martin had the day off, and that it was her sister speaking. It was all very much a family affair. As time went on we could gauge the age of the baby by the snatches of conversation overheard. At first it was 'shh, go to sleep like a good boy'. A few months later it would be 'Albert, do come and help. He's kicked the ink over'. At some later date, when inquiring about a trunk call, it was 'George, if you climb on to that table again you'll get a good smacked bottom'.

Then my sister and I went to France for a year to a so-called finishing school. In our absence the General Post Office bought out the Bell Telephone Company, and Mrs Martin's little front room was no longer our exchange. A combined Post Office and Telephone Exchange had been built around the corner on the main road. We became a number and nothing more.

A Welsh Concert   **by R. G. Whitfield**

It had been announced that the Grand Concert would start at 8.00 p.m., and by that hour the Memorial Hall was packed to capacity. About three hundred people were waiting, chewing sweets, sucking on pipes or shouting tit-bits of local gossip to friends, and the smoky, noisy interior soon resembled a station waiting room at the start of a wakes week pilgrimage.

By ten past eight it had become evident that all we lacked were performers. Boys were despatched with messages, while some ironic hand-clapping and foot-stamping made the message doubly clear. Within a minute came a procession of the Male Voice Choir members from the bar of the Castle Hotel opposite. They walked up the central aisle, bow ties awry and coats in hand, the tenors looking sheepish, the younger basses defiant and the old stagers merely good-humoured. Greetings and friendly insults were exchanged, the froth from the last quick pint was wiped away, and soon they could be half-seen, half-heard, shuffling around behind the curtain.

The Silver Band were made of sterner stuff. Besides, they had a good ten minutes' extra drinking time because they were not needed until after the first few numbers. So for several minutes afterwards men could be heard feeling their way down the darkened auditorium, or creeping past outside. Muttered curses were intermingled with dropped instruments, and one fierce, sibilant interchange ended with 'And you mind where you're putting your trombone, you daft fool!'

But the comedy came to an end, for the Welsh take their music seriously. The noise from the audience gave way to an expectant silence long before the conductor raised his hand. There were thirty-six in the Choir, and they looked as if they could have been anything from farm labourers to bank managers. The wavy hair and flashing eyes of the Celt could be seen; stolid, deeply-lined, dependable faces; huge bronzed men and short, pallid ones; an enormous bass whose seventeen-stone frame was topped by an angelic choir-boy's face.

How they sang! They started quietly enough, feeling their way through the pitch and rhythm of the first two songs. Then, as self-consciousness departed and confidence grew, they sang until the whole building shook and the echoes of the harmonies lingered in the roof. It was the kind of singing which acts on the audience like an electric current − neck, shoulders and scalp tingle, hairs stand out and the sound flows over like a musical tide.

All too soon they had finished. Chaos reigned on stage as thirty-six outgoing choristers found their way blocked by twenty-eight incoming bandsmen. But someone drew the curtains, and one of the tenors came out to keep us amused for five minutes. He told some rather predictable stories about the innate stupidity of tourists, at which the visitors (there must have been at least six of us) smiled dutifully, while the locals laughed uproariously.

Then the Band was revealed − looking rather different from the Choir, whose white shirts and maroon bow ties had given them a pleasantly uniform appearance. The trombonists, it is true, were impeccably dressed and managed to appear slightly aloof throughout the whole proceedings (even to the point of being half a beat out in one of the trickier passages and glaring at the conductor as if he were out of time). But the rest of the Band came as the spirit moved them, in shirt-sleeves, pullovers, jeans and even a leather jacket. There was nothing casual about their playing. What they lacked in finesse they made up for in intensity. What they lacked in skill was unimportant beside the enthusiasm that replaced it. They threw themselves into 'Semper Fidelis' at a pace and volume that left both audience and performers gasping; and throughout a repertoire which took in folk songs, classical arrangements and hymn tunes they played with a commitment so total that I wanted to stand up and cheer.

Fortunately, others felt the same way, so we were able to express our feelings at the end.

The conductor was an unforgettable character. Short, stocky and grey-haired, he refused absolutely to be impressed or intimidated by his men. In his left hand he carried a trumpet, joining in when things got tricky, and in his right the baton. Unfortunately, years of obviously successful conducting had left him not only supremely competent, but also stone deaf. The result was often hilarious, sometimes incredible. To mark a change of time he would beat his baton against the music stand, or his instrument, the noise reminding one irresistibly of a small boy with a wooden spoon and a saucepan. To give instruction he disdained gestures and grimaces, but simply bellowed the loudest stage whispers I have ever heard, so that all of us were ready for the entrances, and shared in the expressions of wrath. Yet Band and Choir between them held us entranced for two hours. Solo items provided a breathing space, nothing more, while the others sought renewed energy (principally, it seemed, from bottles of Guinness).

Finally the concert finished with the audience joining in. Almost inevitably, the last song was 'Cwm Rhondda'. I sang as loudly as my next-door neighbour, and the fact that he sang in Welsh and I in English mattered not at all. At the end, red-faced and breathless, we grinned at each other. Then he held out his hand to shake mine and said, 'Nothing like a good sing, bach!' I knew he was right.

My Country Cottage   by Stella Gibbons

I do not know who called my cottage Weavers Whim nor do I care. Dooer, the dark pantherine man who lives in a huddled squalor of huts behind a knot of hazel bushes opposite my cottage, says that it has always been called Weavers Whim, or just Weavers. But that would not do, of course; it was too sickeningly Barrie-ish. I got Bim down, the day after I bought it, and Bim put The Wen – just The Wen, not a word more – on the gate in chromium lettering. We *had* fun doing it. We got very dirty pulling the beams about and Bim sweated a lot and we stripped the walls and Bim began a fresco on

Birds in Winter

by Arnold Wiles

'They should keep the herons from eyeing the goldfish'

'Can't recall seeing such a large flock of redwings and fieldfares before'

'Looks like being another hard winter for the birds'

'Perhaps we should draw the curtains until after I've carved'

them, a sort of interpretation of the landscape outside, dark and lowering and bluey-purple.

Dooer came and lunged, tigerishly, in the doorway while we were doing it.

'Do you like it?' we asked him, just to see how he would react.

He looked at it for a long time and then he said, 'No'.

That moved me. It makes me rather sad to remember how much it moved me, because Dooer has been a disappointment. After he had been in three times to see if there was anything he could do, and we said no unless you just stay with us and we have fun together. Dooer said well, he had some work to do, *he* had, and went off and presently we saw him digging in the dullest way in a bit of garden he has, while the wireless played and chickens ran about.

I do think chickens are *dull*.

But the cottage went on being fun. We had Oofy and Pug and Noel and Tessa down for the week-end and made them dig, and they hated it. We got sick of Bim's fresco, so we stripped it off and washed the walls a heavenly surrealist pale ox-blood. Then we got an awful cramped feeling; we just felt we would die if we didn't have space, so we pulled down the wall between the sitting-room and the dining-room to make one marvellous big room where we could lie and listen to the gramophone.

Then the ceiling fell down. I rushed over to find Dooer, and he was asleep in front of the fire with the Sunday paper all over him. He said, 'What du yer expect, playin' the fool with the place?' and he came over and looked at it and shook his head.

'I'll get a man down from London', I said.

'Shall the missus bring you over a broom?' said Dooer.

What fun! we hadn't got a broom. So Mrs Dooer brought one over, and we had the most marvellous time *sweeping*. We were just like children over it, laughing and running out to pick branches and crowning ourselves, only Pug got cross because Noel would crown Oofy and not him, and then we all got tired, so we made some tea and talked and talked and talked until three in the morning. The *stillness* was so strange. Then we all went to bed.

Next morning the kitchen fell in. Dooer came over, and shook his head again.

'Oh', I said, 'don't fuss. I'll get a man down to strip and pickle the whole place, and we'll have a tiny water-garden, all Persian, with a Walk, and Oofy can cut the bushes into symbolic shapes'. Dooer didn't say anything. Presently I saw him talking to the Vicar, an awful, repressed looking man with an hysterical roar of laughter that *couldn't* be normal. Oofy had to see a man in town and we ran out of money so we couldn't buy any more drink and so we all went back.

I really must go down next week-end and see about the cottage. Pug left some books there and the place must be in an awful muddle. Perhaps Tiggy would run me down in her car. I really *must*.

Winter Tail Corn

A PARTY of Norfolk men who were employed beating for the pheasant shoot had to cross a dyke between two fenland fields. When one of them landed in the water he explained, 'Ah leapt a'right but Ah lit too soon'.

FIRST things first. An old carter saw me one harvest time stooking sheaves of corn which were infested with thistles. I was wearing a jacket and the old fellow asked if I was cold. On being told that the jacket was to protect my arms from the thistles, he retorted, 'Your arms will heal up, your coat won't'.

YORKSHIRE farmer's response to complaint about midges, 'Ay, when ye kill one, a thousand cum t't'funeral'.

DERBYSHIRE woman, surveying a scene of confusion and indecision, 'Ee! They're like the four that went five abreast!'

WEATHER prophet at Herefordshire show, glancing up at bank of threatening cloud: 'It d' look tarrble quarrelsome up there'.

LINCOLNSHIRE woman, explaining old friend's previous occupation as midwife: 'She was a bairn-catcher'.

The Season of the Year

by Arnold Wiles

'All you think about is
your stomach'

'I'll say this for Henry – he certainly knows how to make the best of things'

'Try to look wise!'

'The Archers: an everyday story of country folk'

AN old man was pulling down a window blind when the whole lot suddenly came down. Said he, 'I've pulled that blind down hundreds of times, and never pulled it down once!'

ATTENDANT at Irish race meeting, helping motorist to park his car, 'Go ahead, back away'.

OLD countryman after an illness, resentful of being told he is looking better: 'Eh, mebbee, but a reead coo can be just as badly as a white un'.

DEVONSHIRE woman, of newcomers to the village: 'They'm all posh-like, look 'ee − 'aves their vorenoons [elevenses] at ten-thirty 'stead o' nine'.

EXTOLLING the intelligence of her cat, an old Wiltshire woman explained: ''E's that bright 'e could talk, but 'e won't for feared I should send 'im to shop'.

SCOTS woman, describing beggar's attire: 'He hadna as much on him as would stuff a stilt' [pad a crutch].

GRANDDAUGHTER, aged eight, on seeing the first wasps of summer, remarked: 'Last year Grandad gave me 5p for every wasps' nest I found. This year it will be 10p, with VAT'.

NURSE overheard in a Norfolk hospital: 'Right you be then; I'll send for the doctor, but I hope you're bad enough'.

LANCASHIRE woman, learning that a relative had received a £25 Premium Bond prize two weeks before her death and that another £250 prize had arrived shortly after her funeral: 'Ee by gum, wasn't she lucky!'

FROM a Cumberland woman's account of a meeting: 'Then in cumt yon girt orkered lass o' Bessie Brown's, in a new 'at an' coat, stalks reet into t' front row an' sits pruning 'ersel' like a peacock'.

RURAL grocer, of rival in larger village: 'He's got a nice business there; plenty of chimneypots to support him'.

SCOTTISH woman describing local gossip, 'She'd talk a gramophone to scrap iron, that one'.

A SLIP fielder took a very good catch on a south Derbyshire cricket ground. One of the locals, surprised and delighted, shouted 'Ay doave end ketched it!'

OVERHEARD on a Buckinghamshire railway station, a man explaining why he was still working when his three children were all now at work: 'Well, yer don't see the chick scratch for the 'en, do yer?'

OLD man's comment on very spoiled youth: 'What can you expect? He's been reared in a top hat on the side of the grate'.

BORDER worthy, discussing unpopular parish minister: 'Ye could wipe a' the releegion off yon maun wi' a strae wusp an' no' be sair laid oan'.

DORSET builder, recommending a firm of scrap merchants: 'Oh, they're a good firm and very well known; you often see their name in the paper for buying stolen things'.

WILTSHIRE local, being asked where someone lived in the village: 'If thee could tell I his Mother's name before she be wed, then I could tell thee where he lives now'.

'I haven't much hope for the hay, either'

by Brian Walker

'This weather makes me sick'

by Hywel